How to Rent a
FIRE
LOOKOUT
in the
Pacific Northwest

A guide to renting fire lookouts, guard stations, ranger cabins, warming shelters, and bunkhouses in the National Forests of OREGON and WASHINGTON

Tish McFadden
Tom Foley

WILDERNESS PRESS

❧

How to Rent a
Fire Lookout
in the
Pacific
Northwest

A guide to renting fire lookouts, guard stations,
ranger cabins, warming shelters and bunkhouses
in the National Forests of
OREGON and WASHINGTON

Tish McFadden
Tom Foley

WILDERNESS PRESS ... *on the trail since 1967*
BERKELEY, CA

How to Rent a Fire Lookout in the Pacific Northwest

1st EDITION 1996
2nd EDITION 2005
  Second Printing 2006

Front cover photos copyright © 2005 by Tish McFadden and Tom Foley
Frontispiece photo copyright © 2005 by Tom Foley
Maps: Ben Pease, Pease Press
Cover design: Lisa Pletka
Book design: Lisa Pletka
Book editor: Jessica Benner

All new material in this second edition was researched, compiled, and written
by Tish McFadden.

ISBN 978-0-89997-384-5

Manufactured in the United States of America
Distributed by Publishers Group West

Published by: **Wilderness Press**
              1345 8th Street
              Berkeley, CA 94710
              (800) 443-7227; FAX (510) 558-1696
              info@wildernesspress.com
              www.wildernesspress.com

Visit our website for a complete listing of our books and for ordering
information.

Cover photos: *main photo:* Pickett Butte Lookout, Umpqua National
                  Forest (Tish McFadden); *top inset:* Hamma Hamma Cabin,
                  Olympic National Forest (Tom Foley); *middle inset:* Bald
                  Butte Lookout, Fremont National Forest (Tish McFadden);
                  bottom inset: Interrorem Cabin, Olympic National Forest
                  (Tom Foley)

Frontispiece: Warner Mountain Lookout, Willamette National Forest

Notice: Although Wilderness Press and the authors have made every
attempt to ensure that the information in this book is accurate at press time,
they are not responsible for any loss, damage, injury, on inconvenience that
may occur to anyone while using this book. Be aware that many of the roads
described in this book are not well maintained or patrolled, and that road
conditions can change from day to day. Check with the appropriate author-
ities before visiting any of these properties.

Dedication

Lovingly dedicated to my sons, Joel and Logan Steinfeld, whose own life journey now beckons; to my sister Laurie McFadden, with whom I've shared the journey since childhood; and to my mother, Patricia McFadden, who tenderly started me on the journey nearly fifty years ago.

Tish McFadden

Acknowledgments

A project such as this could not be completed without the help of a great many people—so many that to make a list of their names would take several pages. But we must thank Bruce Nichols of Bly Ranger District— without his help this book might not exist; Cherie Leonardo, also of Bly Ranger District; Catherine Callaghan of Lakeview Ranger District; Jackie McConnell of Bear Valley Ranger District; Brenda Taylor and Mel Ford of Barlow Ranger District; Susan Graham of Hood Canal Ranger District; Janel Lacy of Heppner Ranger District; Mike Keown of Illinois Valley Ranger District; and Harvey Timeus and Angie Dillingham of Chetco Ranger District.

Also, our heartfelt thanks to David Steinfeld, Veronica and Nino Foley, Don Harriss, Charlotte Hadella, Ralph Hartman, Pat McFadden, Gail Throop, Kevin Peer, and Thomas Doty, who assisted in a multitude of ways—from the practical to the philosophical. Our special thanks to poet Gary Snyder, a former fire-lookout guard, who graciously allowed us to include his poems, as well as to Angelika Thusius and Yvonne Rose-Merkle. Thanks also to Brian and Cathy Freeman, of Crystal Castle Graphics, for their generosity in sharing their expertise.

Our thanks to the US Forest Service personnel who renovate and preserve these rustic structures and make them available for public use. And our thanks too, to the many community volunteers who donate time, materials, and support to this rare cause.

Tish McFadden
Tom Foley
January, 2005

Overview Oregon and Washington Rental Cabins

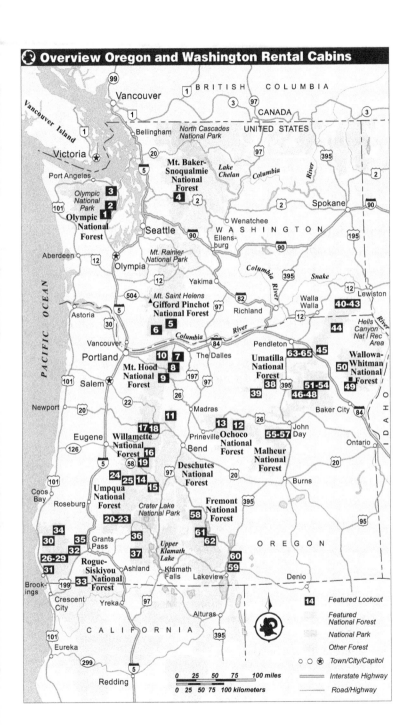

Featured Lookout
Featured National Forest
National Park
Other Forest
Town/City/Capitol
Interstate Highway
Road/Highway

0 25 50 75 100 miles
0 25 50 75 100 kilometers

Table of Contents

Preface

> *"It is surprising how many great men and women a small house will contain."*
>
> Henry David Thoreau, *Walden*

One clear night, I gazed down upon twinkling stars from the catwalk of a lookout tower. With the horizon curving under my watch, the night canopy appeared bright, intimate, and comforting. Mystified, I felt very small here, yet boundless—held for a brief, solitary moment by the greatness of our universe.

* * *

As I ascended the final rise to find a glass house and flagpole on a sage-brush summit, I felt only a portion of the delight which was yet to come. Later that night a thick snowfall danced in a cold September wind and thunder rocked mountains to the west. Lithe snows, lit by a heavenly light. Fog followed. I slept in comfort in the clouds in a little house on a rounded mountaintop breathing the sage and pine-scented air at 7500 feet.

At midnight, I was up to drink water and wander outside. A staggering sight took my breath and made me dizzy—a clear sky and a cosmos so rich and deep, dark and near—I swayed at the sight. Familiar constellations magnified by altitude and brightened by these wilderness surroundings loomed overhead like a celestial Sistine Chapel. Oh wholly night.

* * *

Bound pages of weather worn journals are often found in a drawer or on a tabletop in the fire lookouts and cabins described in this book. Sometime during your stay, crack one open and be prepared to meet some of the most delicious characters you will ever encounter. Words pour to the pages from hearts and souls of real people who have slept here before you; discover their sketches, poetry, observations, yearnings, and dreams. From these cabin renters' logs glow vivid impressions, experiences, and insights of past travelers—artists, scientists, writers, hikers, and back-country wanderers of all ages who now have something in common with you: the choice made for a conscious pause on this mountaintop, removed from the hurried pace of every-day living. As a guest, you are becoming part of the continuing story of this remote and wild place you are privileged, at least for this night, to call home.

* * *

My own affection for these historic structures peppered throughout the National Forests of the Pacific Northwest began before 1980, the year I moved to Oregon as a cultural anthropologist and historian for the US Forest Service. Prior to my arrival, I worked in the Intermountain Region where I first encountered fire lookout towers. I listed the Ute Mountain Fire Lookout on the National Register of Historic Places as my last official act in Utah and I was eager to continue this work in Southern Oregon. It was, however, not in my official capacity as a federal employee that this book was launched or conceived. For this I wish to thank Tom Foley, the United States Forest Service, and the editors at Wilderness Press.

—Tish McFadden,
January, 2005

Quick Reference Chart

Rental	National Forest	Season Available	Cost/ Night	Max Capacity	Page No.
1. Hamma Hamma Cabin	Olympic	Year-round	$40	6	7
2. Interrorem Ranger Cabin	Olympic	Year-round	$30	4	10
3. Louella Cabin	Olympic	Year-round	$40	6	14
4. Evergreen Mountain LO	Snoqualmie	Aug-Nov	$40	4	17
5. Peterson Prairie GS	Gifford-Pinchot	Year-round	$50	6	21
6. Gov. Mineral Spings GS	Gifford-Pinchot	Year-round	$65	9	23
7. Fivemile Butte LO	Mount Hood	Year-round	$30	4	27
8. Flag Point LO	Mount Hood	Nov-May	$30	4	31
9. Clear Lake LO	Mount Hood	Nov-May	$30	4	34
10. Lost Lake Cabins	Mount Hood	May-Oct	$45-100	15	36
11. Green Ridge LO	Deschutes	Apr-June	$30	4	41
12. Cold Springs GS	Ochoco	May-Oct	$50	8	45
13. Lookout Mtn Bunks	Ochoco	Nov-Mar	$60	8	47
14. Warner Mountain LO	Willamette	Nov-May	$40	4	51
15. Timpanogas Shelter	Willamette	July-Oct	$40	8	54
16. Indian Ridge LO	Willamette	July-Sept	$40	4	55
17. Fish Lake Commis.	Willamette	Nov-Mar	$40	4	58
18. Fish Lake Hall House	Willamette	Nov-Mar	$60	4	60
19. Box Canyon GS	Willamette	June-Sept	$40	6	61
20. Acker Rock LO	Umpqua	June-Oct	$40	4	65
21. Pickett Butte LO	Umpqua	Nov-May	$40	4	68
22. Whisky Camp	Umpqua	June-Oct	$40	8	70
23. Butler Butte Cabin	Umpqua	Year-round	$40	8	72
24. Fairview Peak LO Tower	Umpqua	June-Oct	$40	4	74
25. Musick GS	Umpqua	June-Oct	$40	10	77
26. Snow Camp LO	Siskiyou	May-Oct	$30	5	81
27. Packers Cabin	Siskiyou	Year-round	$20	10	85
28. Ludlum House	Siskiyou	Year-round	$40	30	87
29. Quail Prairie LO	Siskiyou	June-Oct	$50	4	90
30. Lake of the Woods LO	Siskiyou	May-Oct	$40	4	92
31. Rainbow Creek Tent	Siskiyou	June-Oct	$10	10	94

Rental	National Forest	Season Available	Cost/ Night	Max Capacity	Page No.
32. Pearsoll Peak LO	Siskiyou	June-Sept	no fee	4	95
33. Bolan Mountain LO	Siskiyou	July-Oct	$40	4	99
34. Bald Knob LO	Siskiyou	May-Oct	$35	4	100
35. Onion Mountain LO	Siskiyou	May-Oct	$40	4	102
36. Imnaha Cabin	Rogue River	Year-round	$40	6	103
37. Willow Prairie Cabin	Rogue River	Year-round	$15	4	105
38. Ditch Creek GS	Umatilla	Year-round	$40	6	109
39. Tamarack LO Cabin	Umatilla	Year-round	$25	4	111
40. Clearwater LO Cabin	Umatilla	Year-round	$25	4	114
41. Clearwater Bighouse Cabin	Umatilla	Year-round	$40-$60	10	116
42. Godman GS	Umatilla	Year-round	$40-$60	8	117
43. Wenatchee GS	Umatilla	Year-round	$30	4	119
44. Fry Meadow GS	Umatilla	Year-round	$25	4	122
45. Summit GS Bunkhouse	Umatilla	Year-round	$35	4	125
46. Miner's Retreat	Umatilla	Year-round	$30-$50	6	127
47. Congo Gulch Cabin	Umatilla	Year-round	$50	6	130
48. Hilltop Hideaway	Umatilla	Year-round	$30	2	132
49. Two Color GS	Wallowa-Whitman	Year-round	$60-160	12	137
50. Moss Springs GS	Wallowa-Whitman	Year-round	$60-$70	5	139
51. Antlers GS	Wallowa-Whitman	Year-round	$40	6	141
52. Peavy Cabin	Wallowa-Whitman	July-Mar	$40	6	143
53. Anthony Lakes GS	Wallowa-Whitman	May-Oct	$80-$90	8	146
54. Boundary GS	Wallowa-Whitman	Year-round	$40-$100	8	148
55. Murderer's Creek	Malheur	May-Nov	$40	4	151
56. Fall Mountain LO	Malheur	June-Sept	$40	2	154
57. Deer Creek GS	Malheur	May-Nov	$40	4	156
58. Hager Mountain LO	Silver Lake	Nov-April	$25	4	159
59. Aspen Cabin	Fremont	June-Oct	$25	4	162
60. Drake Peak LO	Fremont	July-Oct	$25	4	164
61. Currier GS	Fremont	June-Nov	$30	4	166
62. Bald Butte LO	Fremont	June-Oct	$30	2	168
63. Totem Bunkhouse	Oregon SP	Year-round	$20	4	173
64. One-Room Rustic Cabins	Oregon SP	Year-round	$35	4	175
65. Two-Room Rustic Cabins	Oregon SP	Year-round	$35	6	177

Walking

It is true, we are but faint-hearted crusaders, even the walkers, nowadays, who undertake no persevering, never-ending enterprises. Our expeditions are but tours, and come round again at evening to the old hearthside from which we set out. Half the walk is but retracing our steps. We should go forth on the shortest walk, perchance, in the spirit of undying adventure, never to return, prepared to send back our embalmed hearts only as relics to our desolate kingdoms. If you are ready to leave father and mother, and brother and sister, and wife and child and friends, and never see them again—if you have paid your debts, and made your will, and settled all your affairs, and are a free man—then you are ready for a walk.

— Henry David Thoreau, *Walking*

Enjoying Your Adventure

Safety

We urge readers to use common sense when evaluating their hiking and skiing skills. If we say a hike is arduous, it may be impossible for some though easy for others. If we say the road is rough, leave the Maserati at home. Skiing to some of these places in a winter snowstorm might be thrilling for some but fatal for others. You will usually find at least one knowledgeable person at every Ranger District who will give you the information you need about weather, access, road conditions, snow depth, and difficulties you are likely to encounter at any particular time of year.

Always be well-prepared when entering the backcountry, especially in wintertime. Carry tire chains and a shovel. During a typical winter you may be traveling on skis or snowshoes for as much as ten miles or as little as a few hundred yards, depending on your particular destination. A longer trip can be extremely difficult in snow and could take an entire day. Plan accordingly and start early. Although there might be clear road access to the cabin or lookout on your way in, a heavy over-night snowfall could leave you stranded there, even in late fall or early spring. Be prepared. Carry extra clothing in waterproof containers. Be sure to notify someone of your destination, including departure and return dates.

If you intend bringing young children to a fire-lookout tower, please inquire from the managing Ranger District whether it is safe to do so. Some of the lookouts are ideal for children of any age, while others, because of their height, steep stairways, and precipitous, rocky surroundings are not.

Occasionally, during strong winds, lookout towers may sway slightly. Don't worry, they are built to do this. It is safer to remain in the tower than to attempt to descend the stairway during lightning or a wind storm. The lookout is well grounded...you may not be.

Many of the lookouts and cabins are equipped with propane appliances—heating, cooking, lighting. Use caution when using these and please remember to turn them off completely when leaving.

Water

Most lookouts and cabins do not have safe drinking water, and many have no water at all. Cleaning and washing water can sometimes be obtained from streams or melting snow; however, safe drinking water cannot be assured unless it is purified, filtered, or boiled for five minutes. If you are bringing water, we suggest a gallon per day per person.

Lookouts

At most lookouts you will find the Osborne Fire Finder, a standard piece of equipment for observing and mapping smoke and wildfire. You are welcome to use it—with great care—for identifying landmarks and natural features of the area.

Rental Conditions

The Forest Service is eager to point out that it is not interested in the motel business. You will find no bed linen at any of these rentals—you may not find mattresses in some places—you will not find towels or chocolate mints on your pillow, in fact, you will not find any pillow. In most places there is no potable water—until you purify it—often no sink, and only in a few places will you find electricity or plumbing.

Reservations

Forest Service recreational rentals throughout the Pacific Northwest Region are unifying their cabin and lookout reservation system in 2005. All available rentals are to be reserved through the National Recreation Reservation Service. To make a reservation for any listed properties in this book, with the exception of the Emigrant Springs State Park listings, call toll free: 1-877-444-6777 or reserve online at www.ReserveUSA.com. You will be asked to provide the following information when you make your reservation: facility name, arrival and departure dates, the number of people in your party, and method of payment. A reservation fee is added to the cost of your rental reservation.

The rentals are available on a first-come, first-served basis. Some Ranger Districts have specific check-in/checkout times, some do not. We specify those that do. Some Ranger Districts limit the duration of your stay to three nights, others allow as many as ten, others are undecided. We specify this information wherever possible. Check with the managing Ranger District.

For some rentals, such as Hamma Hamma, Interrorem, Two Color, Lost Lake, and Snow Camp, you may need to make reservations up to ten months in advance, particularly on holiday weekends, however, advanced reservations are required for all rentals.

The rental fee for each structure is used exclusively for the maintenance of that particular structure, and is not lost, as you might expect, in the black hole of bureaucracy. Some Ranger Districts require a deposit, others do not. We specify those that do. If your plans change you may request a rental refund or a credit transfer, but you must do so at least three weeks before your reservation date. If the Forest Service determines the weather conditions are too severe for you to reach the rental safely, you will be given credit toward the next available date.

Remember to Bring

See the Must Have list below. Most cabins and lookouts are well sup-plied with a heat source, pots and pans, and eating utensils, though a few are not. Inquire at the managing Ranger District office. You will need the items listed in the Must Have section at all rentals. Our What to Bring heading for each structure includes only those items needed for that par-ticular structure—though we always mention water where it is necessary.

Responsible Use

Please leave the cabin or lookout as you found it, or as you would like to have found it. Leave all pots, pans, and utensils clean and ready for the next guests. Sweep the floor, pack out garbage, turn off all appliances, lights, and propane, and lock the door.

If you are renting a lookout in the winter please leave the catwalk and steps clear of snow.

If you bring pets, make sure they don't disturb wildlife, and please clean up after them. If you bring stock animals, keep them tethered when not in use, and bring weed-free feed for them.

If you bring stoves or lanterns, we suggest propane fuel since it burns cleaner than liquid gas.

Most of these lookouts and cabins already have an established fire ring. Please use it; do not establish another. Campfires are a luxury. Please be kind to the woods by keeping your fire very small.

Hunters, please hang your kill outdoors (on meat poles when provid-ed); please, please do not butcher any part of an animal in the cabin; and please pack out every last bit, leaving the area just as you found it.

Finally, no shooting within a quarter mile of these rentals.

Note

The directions to each property in this book were provided by the Forest Service and have not all been authenticated by the authors. Due to ever-changing road names and numbers on Forest Service lands in the Pacific Northwest, and seasonal road closures, it is imperative that read-ers to consult knowledgeable Ranger District personnel and appropriate maps prior to each trip in order to get the most current information.

Since the first printing of this guidebook in 1996, the roster of lookouts, cabins, and guard stations in the USFS Recreation Rental Program has soared. Although 11 listings from the original book are off line, 34 new listings are included in this second edition for Oregon and Washington alone. According to Ranger District reports, the number of Forest Service rental structures will continue to expand. For the latest listings, added to the program since the 2005 printing, consult Ranger District offices or Forest Service websites.

What to Bring

We always forget something when we plan for a trip—or we bring too much—but that is part of the experience of traveling. This list may help you decide what to bring and what not to bring. Some of these items are supplied at some rentals—check in the "What is Provided" section of the cabin or lookout you are interested in renting.

Must Have

Special Use Permit	Full tank gas
Drinking water and/or water filter	This guidebook
Food	Flashlight
Toilet paper	Good tires
Waterproof matches	Area/topographic maps
Garbage bags	Extra batteries & bulb
Sunglasses	Spare tire
Pocket knife	Sunburn protection
Rental key	Clothing (dress for extremes)
Sleeping bags	Change tire kit
Axe and shovel	Hat
First-aid kit	Whistle
Sleeping pads	Compass

Nice To Have

Bug repellent
Ground coffee or tea bags
Bar soap
Day pack
Extra blankets
Dish towel
Salt and pepper
Pillows
Dish washing soap
Picnic cooler
Small gas stove (some places a must)
Water bucket
Eating utensils
Towels
Dishes, pots and pans
  (some places a must)
Lantern (some places a must)
Rope
Candles
Backpack

Useful Extras

Bikes
Pens and pencils
Nature guides
Binoculars
Writing pad
Star guide
Camera
Sketch pad, watercolors
Books
Musical instrument
Playing cards

Map Legend

Map Legend

19	Rental Cabin Described in This Chapter
24	Rental Cabin Described in Another Chapter
River or Stream	
Body of Water	
Featured National Forest	
Adjacent National Forest	
Wilderness Area	
National Park	

=====	Freeway or Interstate
———	Major Road
········	Minor Road
– – – –	Gravel Road
(5)	Interstate Highway
(2)	U.S. Highway
(4)	State Highway
(S5)	County Highway
[18]	Forest Highway
[1234]	Other Route
○ ○ ✱	Town/City/Capitol City
▲	Peak

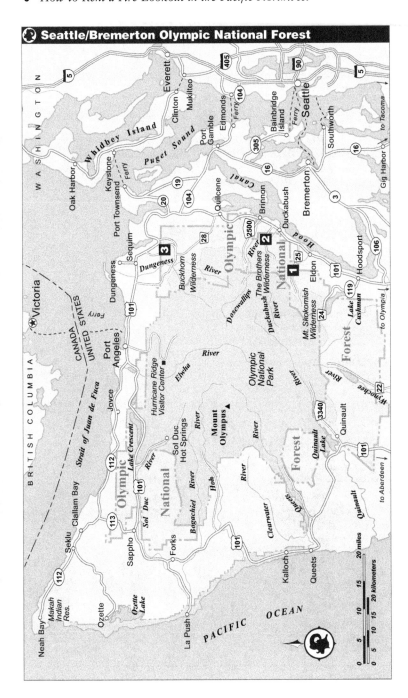

Seattle/Bremerton Olympic National Forest

Olympic National Forest

"I feel that as long as the Earth can make a spring every year, I can. As long as the Earth can flower and produce nurturing fruit, I can, because I'm the Earth. I won't give up until the Earth gives up."

Alice Walker

1 Hamma Hamma Cabin

YOUR BEARINGS

50 miles northwest of Olympia
70 miles west of Seattle, approximately (via ferry)
75 miles northwest of Tacoma
170 miles north of Portland

AVAILABILITY Year-round, weather permitting.

CAPACITY Six people. No pets.

Hamma Hamma Cabin

DESCRIPTION Single-story cabin with gabled and hipped roof lines. Living room, kitchen, two bedrooms, full bath. A delightful and very popular lodge in a beautiful setting.

COST $40 per night plus reservation fee. $25 refundable deposit is required.

RESERVATIONS Call the toll-free National Recreation Reservation Service at 1-877-444-6777 or make reservations online at www.ReserveUSA.com.

HOW TO GET THERE The road is paved all the way. During the winter months access may be limited to cross-country skis and snowshoes for the final four miles, though Hood River Ranger District tells us this happens only rarely. Consult them regarding current road and snow conditions prior to your departure.

From Hoodsport, travel 14 miles north on US Highway 101 to Forest Road 25. Turn left. The sign reads hamma hamma recreation area. Continue on the Hamma Hamma Road six miles to a driveway on the right. Watch for the sign on the right: HAMMA HAMMA CABIN: OCCU-PIED RESIDENCE. The cabin is about 100 yards up this driveway. The access road is gated; please respect the renter's privacy. To view the cabin, walk the Living Legacy Nature Trail.

ELEVATION 560 feet

WHAT IS PROVIDED Living room, kitchen, two bedrooms, one bathroom with flush toilet. The only water available is to the toilet. Bring your own water for drinking, cooking and household uses. Potable water is available from a hand pump well at Lena Creek Campground two miles west on Forest Service Road 25 during the recreation use season (June-September). Propane heater, cook range, refrigerator, and lights. Propane is furnished. Inquire at Hoodsport office for accessibility for individuals with disabilities.

WHAT TO BRING Drinking water, or the means to treat the local water. Bring camping supplies as well as garbage bags (pack it in, pack it out), candles or a lantern for emergencies, first aid kit, sleeping bag/bedding, toiletries, washcloths and towels, dish soap, and bar soap.

THE SETTING If a contest were held to decide the most sought-after rental cabin in this book, Hamma Hamma would be the certain winner, and the runner up would surely be its sister cabin on the Olympic Peninsula, Interrorem.

There are compelling reasons for this popularity, beyond the prox-imity to Seattle. Hamma Hamma is a rare and delightful place where one easily feels at home and at peace. It is more akin to a lodge than a cabin; its lovely living room is embraced by a semicircle of bay windows overlooking the Hamma Hamma River drainage.

HISTORY The skill and craftsmanship of the Civilian Conservation Corps, which constructed this fine Guard Station during 1936 and 1937, have earned Hamma Hamma Cabin a nomination to the National Register of Historic Places.

We were intrigued by the origin and meaning of the name "Hamma Hamma." Having dismissed our suggestion that it was of porcine origin, possibly the name of a Native pork pie, the ever-resourceful Susie Graham of the Hood Canal Ranger District told us that, originally, it was thought to be the Twana Indian name for "Stinky Stinky," but that further research indicates that it may be the Twana Indian name of the root of a rush that grows in the area.

Local Girl Scouts have undertaken the maintenance of the cabin since March 1992. Please help them by keeping the site as you found it—or, at least, as you would like to have found it.

AROUND YOU The Olympic Peninsula and Hood Canal. To the west is Mt. Skokomish Wilderness; to the northwest, Brothers Wilderness; to the east, Hood Canal. Two miles west on Road 25 is the trailhead for Lena Lake, Trail 810. There is parking, a vault toilet and well water at Lena Creek Campground. It is less than three miles to the lake—and the junction with Trail 811, which takes you to Upper Lena Lake—and 3.5 miles to the junction with Brother Trail 821, which takes you several miles into Brothers Wilderness.

To reach Skokomish Wilderness, continue west from Hamma Hamma Cabin on Road 25 for about six miles to access Putvin Trail 813, classed as "most difficult." Or travel eight miles west to Trail 822, also classed as "most difficult," which leads to Mildred Lakes, 4.5 miles from Hoodsport.

FOR MORE INFORMATION
Hood Canal Ranger District—Hoodsport Office
P.O. Box 68, Hoodsport, WA 98548
(360) 877-5254
http://www.fs.fed.us/r6/olympic/recreation-nu/cabins_1.shtml

"Now that I've refilled my heart and soul with the inspiration and tranquility of the forest, I can return to Seattle, normal."

From the Cabin's Guestbook

2 Interrorem Ranger Cabin

YOUR BEARINGS

60 miles northwest of Olympia
75 miles west of Seattle
75 miles northwest of Tacoma
180 miles northwest of Portland

AVAILABILITY Year-round.

CAPACITY A maximum of four people. No pets.

DESCRIPTION Historic, single-story, 24 x 20-foot, peeled-log cabin with kitchen, living room, bedroom, open porch, and pyramidal cedar-shake roof. It is sturdy and honest, with an appealing gray hue, as though proud of its venerable age.

COST $30 per night plus reservation fee. $25 refundable deposit is required.

Interrorem Ranger Cabin

RESERVATIONS Call the toll-free National Recreation Reservation Service at 1-877-444-6777, or make reservations online at www.ReserveUSA.com. Visit the Olympic National Forest website for more regional information: www.fs.fed.us/r6/olympic.

HOW TO GET THERE Travel 22 miles north of Hoodsport on US Highway 101 to the Duckabush Recreation Area. Follow the Duckabush River Road, Road 2510, for four miles to the end of the pavement. Interrorem Ranger Cabin is very pleasantly situated in a fenced yard on the left side of the road just inside the Olympic National Forest boundary.

ELEVATION 300 feet

WHAT IS PROVIDED Propane fridge, cook range, heater, and lights. Propane fuel is provided. The kitchen has a vinyl floor, lots of closets, a stove, fridge, and two sinks—though no running water. The bedroom has two bunk beds; the living room has a painted wooden floor, a propane heater, exposed beams, and a table and chairs. Outside is a lovely yard, a picnic table, a vault toilet, a parking area, a barbecue, and a fire-ring. And, if you're lucky, a herd of Roosevelt elk being chased by a friendly cat.

WHAT TO BRING Drinking water and a bucket to bring water from Collins Campground (June to September), or have the means to treat river water. Bring camping supplies as well as garbage bags (pack it in, pack it out), candles or a lantern for emergencies, first aid kit, sleeping bag/bedding, toiletries, washcloths and towels, dish soap, and bar soap.

A Northwest Forest Pass or a Golden Passport is needed to park at the trailhead next to the cabin. When renting the cabin, park your vehicle inside the fence.

HISTORY Emery J. Finch, ranger and Hoodsport pioneer, built the cabin in 1907, and first occupied it with his new bride on April 22, 1908. It was the first administrative office site for Olympic National Forest.

Apart from its role as a honeymoon cabin, Interrorem has also hosted people in several government programs, such as the Emergency Relief Administration, the Works Progress Administration, and the Civilian Conservation Corps. From 1942 to 1986, it had yet another life as a fire-guard station, and from 1986 to 1994 it was used by Forest Service volunteers.

Through an extraordinarily felicitous coincidence the following entry appears in the guestbook to further the cabin's reputation as a honeymoon retreat:

We came here in January for a night and it was beautiful. This time we came back for the start of our honeymoon. We were married July 4th. [This is the day in 1845 that Henry David Thoreau moved into his cabin by Walden Pond. 'Yesterday I came here to live,' he wrote in his journal]. We stayed here July 4th and 5th and enjoyed a much needed rest...so thanks to the Forest Service for providing us with such a beautiful (and inexpensive) place to begin our married life, and we hope you all enjoy it as much as we have, and find it as healing.

The origin and meaning of the name Interrorem are shrouded in the fog of the Olympic Peninsula. Despite its Latin sound, Susie Graham at the Hood Canal Ranger District suggested that it may not be Latin at all but, instead, may be a sly play on words. It seems that, originally, the cabin was built as an interim measure and that, somehow, the word interim became the much grander Interrorem.

AROUND YOU The Olympic Peninsula, Hood Canal, Brothers Wilderness, and Olympic National Park.

From the Duckabush River Road there are lovely views of Brothers Wilderness and the Duckabush River, which may soon be designated a Wild and Scenic River. It is well known for its excellent fishing holes.

Ranger Hole Trail (824) takes off from beside the cabin and is an easy hike down to the Duckabush River, less than one mile away, where the rangers fished and got their household water. Be forewarned about the river, though. It is dangerous—replete with rapids and waterfalls.

The Interrorem Nature Trail (804) is a well-maintained 0.25-mile loop trail off of the Ranger Hole Trail (824). The vegetation here is similar to that found in the Olympic rain forest. There is an abundance of ferns and mosses as well as huge second-growth Douglas-fir and hemlock.

The Duckabush Trail (803) is reached by traveling another two miles west on Forest Road 2510—the Duckabush River Road in front of the cabin. This trail will take you into Brothers Wilderness—one mile from the trailhead and, if you keep going, into Olympic National Park in a distance of 6.8 miles from the trailhead. And if you still haven't had enough, it connects you with other trails within the Park.

As a World Heritage Park, Olympic National Park is in the exalted company of the pyramids of Egypt, Serengeti National Park of Tanzania, and the Great Barrier Reef of Australia. It has the largest and finest example of virgin temperate rain forest in the Western Hemisphere and is one of the few coniferous rain forests in the world. It preserves the largest intact stand of coniferous forest in the contiguous 48 States, and a large herd of Roosevelt elk.

Detailed trail guides are available from the Hood Canal Ranger District. They will gladly mail one to you on request.

FOR MORE INFORMATION
Hood Canal Ranger District—Hoodsport Office
P.O. Box 68, Hoodsport, WA 98548
360-877-5254
http://www.fs.fed.us/r6/olympic/recreation-nu/cabins_1.shtml

August on Sourdough,
a visit from Dick Brewer

You hitched a thousand miles
    north from San Francisco
Hiked up the mountainside a mile in the air

The little cabin—one room—
    walled in glass
Meadows and snowfields, hundred of peaks

We lay in our sleeping bags
    talking half the night;
Wind in the guy-cables   summer mountain rain.

Next morning I went with you
    as far as the cliffs,
Loaned you my poncho—the rain across the shale—

You down the snowfield
    flapping in the wind
Waving a last goodbye   half hidden in the clouds

To go on hitching
    clear to New York;
Me back to my mountain   and far, far, west.

Gary Snyder, *Back Country*

"I know not the first letter of the alphabet. I have always been regretting that I was not as wise as the day I was born."

Henry David Thoreau, *Walden*

3 Louella Cabin

YOUR BEARINGS

3.5 hours south of Seattle

AVAILABILITY Year-round.

CAPACITY 6 people maximum. No pets.

DESCRIPTION Historic Guard Station, built in 1912. Covered front porch affords relaxing views all times of year. Living room furnished with a futon couch that makes into a double bed. Two bedrooms, one with a double bed and one with twin bunk beds.

COST $40 per night plus reservation fee. $25 refundable deposit is required.

RESERVATIONS Call toll-free the National Recreation Reservation Service at 1-877-444-6777 or make reservations online at www.ReserveUSA.com. Visit the Olympic National Forest website for more regional information: www.fs.fed.us/r6/olympic.

HOW TO GET THERE Turn south off Highway 101 onto the Louella road (across from Sequim Bay State Park). Go one mile. Turn left onto Palo Alto Road. Follow Palo Alto Road to Forest boundary where road becomes FS Road 28 (where pavement ends). Drive a short distance to Louella Cabin driveway on right side of road (watch for small sign) and

Louella Cabin

drive past Louella bunkhouse to the rental cabin on the right side of the driveway.

ELEVATION   500 feet

WHAT IS PROVIDED   Kitchen offers table and chairs, cook stove, refrigerator, dishes, posts, silverware, and cooking utensils. Indoor bathroom with shower, sink, and flush toilet. Water, electricity, propane heater, and hot water heater provided. Propane is furnished.

WHAT TO BRING   Bring potable water for cooking, drinking, and washing when water is not available at this cabin. Bring camping supplies as well as garbage bags (pack it in, pack it out), candles or a lantern for emergencies, first aid kit, sleeping bag/bedding, toiletries, washcloths and towels, dish soap, and bar soap.

HISTORY   Forest Service employee, E.M. Cheney, built the Louella Guard Station in 1912. Mr. Cheney dedicated the house to his wife, Louella. A fireguard was stationed here during fire season in the summer and fall. The structures were closed during winter months. During the Great Depression, a Civilian Conservation Corps (CCC) camp was built in the lower part of the meadow below the cabin and consisted of barracks, bathhouse, and a mess hall. After the CCC camp closed in 1939, the cabin was used by other agencies, including the US Army, until 1976. For the subsequent 25 years, Louella Cabin remained unoccupied until it was refurbished and became a part of the Rental Cabin program on the Olympic National Forest.

AROUND YOU   Nearby access to Buckhorn Wilderness Area offers renters opportunities for hiking in beautiful mountain scenery. Fishing is available in the Dungeness and Gray Wolf Rivers. The town of Sequim is 10 miles from the cabin and is the nearest hotspot for supplies.

FOR MORE INFORMATION
Hood Canal Ranger District—Quilcene Office
295142 Highway 101 South
P.O. Box 280
Quilcene, WA 98376
(360) 765-2200
http://www.fs.fed.us/r6/olympic/recreation-nu/cabins_1.shtml

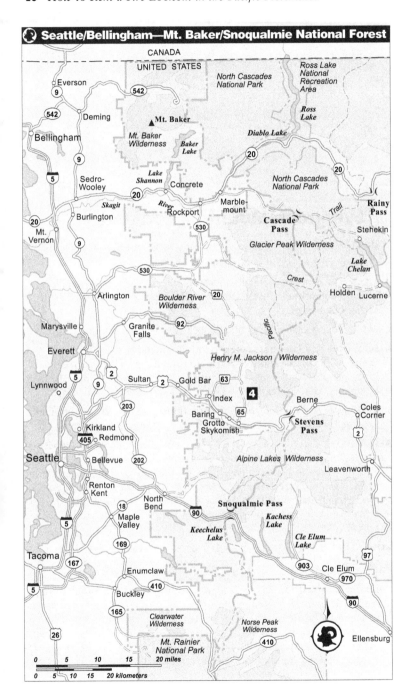

Seattle/Bellingham—Mt. Baker/Snoqualmie National Forest

Snoqualmie National Forest

"The richness I achieve comes from Nature, the source of my inspiration."

Claude Monet

4 Evergreen Mountain Lookout

YOUR BEARINGS

10 miles northeast of Skykomish, Washington

AVAILABILITY August through mid-November is typical, depending on weather conditions. Check with Ranger District for the possibility of an earlier opening date.

CAPACITY Four people maximum, although two would be more comfortable.

DESCRIPTION The Lookout is the ground-mounted L-4 model, 14 x 14 feet in size, with outside shutters and a hip roof design. There is no catwalk. It is perched on a rock overlooking the Evergreen and Beckler Drainages. Glacier Peak can be seen to the north on a clear day.

COST $40 per night. Funds from the rental program will be used to maintain the lookout structure and to administer the rental program.

RESERVATIONS Call the toll-free the National Recreation Reservation Service at 1-877-444-6777 or make reservations online at www.ReserveUSA.com. Visit the Olympic National Forest website for more regional information: http://www.fs.fed.us/r6/mbs/recreation/activities/rentals /evergreen/. Reservations may be made for up to seven consecutive days on a first-come, first-served basis. Check-in time is 2:00 P.M. and checkout time is 1:00 P.M.

HOW TO GET THERE The Lookout is located approximately 10 air miles northeast of the Skykomish Ranger Station. Access to the lookout is a 1.5-mile hike following Forest Service Trail 1056 just off of Forest Service Road 6554. The trail climbs steeply the first 2/3 mile through the old Evergreen Mountain Fire burn of 1967. The trail then enters dense forest while easing the grade a bit until reaching a small saddle below the lookout. The trail then becomes steep again before reaching the lookout. Panoramic views on a clear day include Glacier Peak, Mt. Rainier, and surrounding peaks. The trail is well noted for wildflowers, scenery, and sighting wildlife.

ELEVATION 5587 feet

WHAT IS PROVIDED One twin-sized bed with mattress, three extra mattresses, table, step stool, six folding chairs, a twin burner propane stove, two twin mantle propane lanterns, plates, cups, silverware, serving spoons, sauce pan, two cooking pots, and a large coffee pot. A toilet (outhouse) is located several hundred feet down the ridge from the lookout.

WHAT TO BRING Food and beverages, pillows, bedding or sleeping bags, flashlights with extra batteries, matches, a back-up backpacking stove, bug repellent, garbage bags, camera and extra film, toiletry articles (toilet paper, towels, soap, etc), and your favorite book. There is no water on site. Please carry in enough water for drinking, cooking, and washing needs.

HISTORY The Evergreen Lookout was built in 1935 and was occupied each summer until the early 1980s. The fireguards' primary duties were to detect and report lightning strikes and fires. An instrument called an Osborne Fire Finder was used to accurately detect the fire's location. When a fire was spotted, the fireguard would then call by radio to the Skykomish Ranger Station where firefighters would quickly dispatch to the fire location.

After floodwaters washed out the road leading to the lookout, the Forest Service discontinued regular use of the facility. In 1990 a local volunteer group adopted Evergreen Mountain Lookout and began restoration efforts. During the restoration period the Evergreen Mountain Lookout was placed on the National Register of Historic Places and was nominated for the National Historic Lookout Register. Restoration of the lookout was completed in 2000, and in 2001 the Evergreen Mountain Lookout was added to the Forest Service's Lookout and Cabin Rental Program.

AROUND YOU The Evergreen Mountain Lookout is located adjacent to the Beckler River Watershed. Views of Glacier Peak, Mt. Daniels, Keyes Peak, and Columbia Glacier, and parts of the Henry M. Jackson Wilderness can be seen on a clear day.

FOR MORE INFORMATION
Skykomish Ranger District
74920 NE Stevens Pass Hwy.
P.O. Box 305
Skykomish, WA 98288
(360) 677-2414
http://www.fs.fed.us/r6/mbs/recreation/special/lookouts.shtml
http://www.naturenw.org/cab-mbs.htm

The Tree

This tree, in front of me
Has such presence, in all its essence
Of nature's love of life.

 I close and open and close my eyes
And am filled with delight, surprise.
Tree, are you bending toward me
Or—are you inside me?

 A bird sings high
An insect flies by
And the waterfalls in the little stream
Sound near and far and in-between.
A Tree dream.

Angelika Thusius

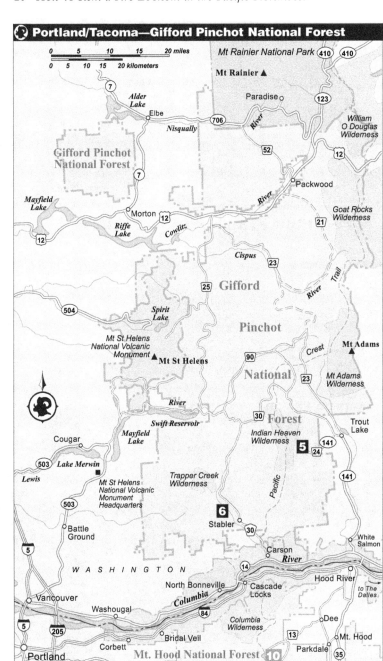

Portland/Tacoma—Gifford Pinchot National Forest

0   5   10   15   20 miles
0   5   10   15   20 kilometers

Mt Rainier National Park

Mt Rainier ▲

Paradise

William O Douglas Wilderness

Gifford Pinchot National Forest

Alder Lake

Elbe

Nisqually

River

Packwood

Mayfield Lake

Morton

Riffe Lake

Cowlitz

River

Goat Rocks Wilderness

Cispus

Gifford

Spirit Lake

Pinchot

Mt St Helens National Volcanic Monument ▲ Mt St Helens

River Trail

Mt Adams ▲

Crest

Mt Adams Wilderness

National

River

Swift Reservoir

Mayfield Lake

Indian Heaven Wilderness

Trout Lake

Forest

Cougar

Lake Merwin

Lewis

Mt St Helens National Volcanic Monument Headquarters

Trapper Creek Wilderness

Pacific

Battle Ground

Stabler

White Salmon

Carson River

W A S H I N G T O N

North Bonneville

Cascade Locks

Hood River

to The Dalles

Vancouver

Washougal

Columbia

Columbia Wilderness

Dee

Bridal Veil

Mt. Hood

Portland

Corbett

Mt. Hood National Forest

Parkdale

O R E G O N

Gifford Pinchot National Forest

"As if you could kill time without injuring eternity."

Henry David Thoreau, *Walden*

5 Peterson Prairie Guard Station

YOUR BEARINGS

10 miles southwest of the town of Trout Lake
35 miles north of the town of Hood River
60 miles northwest of The Dalles
95 miles northeast of Portland

AVAILABILITY Year-round.

CAPACITY The cabin has sleeping accommodations for six people.

Peterson Prairie Guard Station

DESCRIPTION Delightful 18 x 24-foot cabin with bedroom, living room, and small kitchen. There is a lovely old porch at the front, and a smaller one at the back.

COST $50 per night for up to six people.

RESERVATIONS Accepted year-round through www.ReserveAmerica.com up to seven consecutive nights. Two-night minimum on weekends required. Check-in time: 2:00 P.M. Checkout time: 11:00 A.M. Reservations can be made up to a year in advance. Note: ReserveAmerica charges a $9 transaction fee per reservation.

HOW TO GET THERE The cabin is accessible by vehicle on paved roads through late fall for as long as snow conditions allow, and again in the spring after the snow melts. During the snow season skis or snowshoes are required.

From Mount Adams Ranger District, just west of the town of Trout Lake, follow Highway 141 west and southwest for 6.7 miles to Atkisson Sno-Park. Here, at the boundary of Gifford Pinchot National Forest, the highway becomes Forest Road 24. The cabin is 2.5 miles further west on Forest Road 24, on the right side, about 0.25 mile past the main entrance to Peterson Prairie Campground.

Forest Road 24 is closed to wheeled vehicles December 1 through April 1. To leave your vehicle at Atkisson Sno-Park November 15–April 30 requires a Sno-Park permit. Sno-Park permits cost $9 per vehicle for a one-day pass and $21 per vehicle for a season pass. If purchased directly from the State, these permits are $1 less.

ELEVATION 3000 feet

WHAT IS PROVIDED Two futon couches/beds, one double bed, propane cook stove, cooking utensils, propane wall lanterns, woodstove, fire extinguisher, firewood, axe, shovel, broom, and dustpan.

The bedroom, about 8 x 8 feet, has one double bed that sleeps two. The living room has two double futon couches, each accommodating two. The cabin has a fine stone fireplace (with an insert) and chimney, a coffee table, and a small table with four chairs. For lighting, four propane wall lanterns are provided.

The water (located outside of the cabin) is turned on for Memorial Day Weekend, and turned off after Labor Day. A new vault toilet was constructed in back of the cabin in 2004.

WHAT TO BRING Drinking water or the means to treat the local water. We recommend that you have an extra two to three days' supply of food and drinking water as weather may delay your intended departure.

HISTORY This cabin was formerly a fire guard station, built in 1926 on the site of an even older log structure which was used by Forest Service rangers during backcountry patrols.

AROUND YOU   This is a winter recreation area set aside for skiing and snowshoeing. About five miles north on Forest Road 24, near Little Goose Horse Camp, Trail 34 leads west through Indian Heaven Wilderness to the Pacific Crest National Scenic Trail in the heart of the Wilderness.

A trail guide is available at the Ranger District office that gives complete details on more than 50 other trails in the Mt. Adams Ranger District.

FOR MORE INFORMATION
Mt. Adams Ranger District
2455 Hwy 141
Trout Lake, WA 98650
509 395 3400
http://www.fs.fed.us/gpnf/recreation/cabins/index.shtml

———————————————— ————————————————

"I wish to hear the silence of the night, for the silence is something positive and to be heard."
                    Henry David Thoreau, *Journal*, January 21, 1853

6 Government Mineral Springs Guard Station

YOUR BEARINGS
The cabin is located 15 miles north of Carson, Washington

AVAILABILITY Available year-round with a stay limit of seven consecutive days. Reservations can be made up to one year in advance.

CAPACITY The two-story cabin can accommodate nine visitors. No pets are allowed.

DESCRIPTION The cabin has two bedrooms, a kitchen, and living room with a fireplace. The cabin is ideally situated near Trapper Creek Wilderness trailhead and is close to Sno-Parks for winter recreation access. When roads are snow-free, you can reach the cabin by car. During the winter, a trip to the cabin on skis or snowshoes will take you about ten minutes from parking. Propane heat, lights, and cooking range (pots, pans, and dishes) are provided along with wood for the fireplace.

COST $65 per night. There is a two-night minimum over the weekends (Fri-Sat). There is also a $9 reservation fee.

RESERVATIONS Call the toll-free National Recreation Reservation Service at   1-877-444-6777   or   make   reservations   online   at www.ReserveUSA.com. Visit the Gifford Pinchot National Forest website for more regional information: www.fs.fed.us/r6/gpnf.

HOW TO GET THERE From Interstate 84, take the Cascade Locks Exit 44 and cross the Bridge of the Gods (toll bridge) to Hwy 14 in Washington State. Turn east (right) on Hwy 14 and drive five miles to the Carson junction with the Wind River Highway. Follow the Wind River Highway through Carson and northwest approximately 14 miles to the Carson National Fish Hatchery. Continue northwest for one mile on Forest Road 3065 to the entrance for Government Mineral Springs recreation site. From approximately April 15 to November 1, the cabin is usually accessible by vehicle. During the winter season, the cabin is a half-mile trek (skis, snowshoes, or snowmobiles) from the parking area. Sno-Park permits are required from December 1 through April 1. Washington Sno-Park passes are required for Washington State vehicles; out-of-state Sno-Park passes (Idaho, Oregon) will be honored for out-of-state vehicles.

ELEVATION 1200 feet

WHAT IS PROVIDED The lower floor has a large kitchen with a propane stove, a dining room, and a living room with a fireplace and two futon couches that fold down into double beds. Two upstairs bedrooms can accommodate five, with two single beds in one bedroom and one bunk bed that sleeps three in a second bedroom. Propane heat, lights and a cooking stove are provided along with wood for the fireplace. Pots, pans, dishes, and utensils are provided. Bedding and other linens are not

Government Mineral Springs Guard Station

provided. There is no indoor plumbing. The rest room is a vault toilet unit about 150 feet from the cabin.

WHAT TO BRING Camping gear, including bedding and cooking supplies. There is no water available so bring as much as you'll need for drinking, cooking, and washing.

HISTORY This is a newly restored Forest Guard Station, originally built in 1937 by the Civilian Conservation Corps—nestled in a grove of towering old-growth firs.

AROUND YOU The cabin is located between Mount St. Helens and the Columbia River Gorge National Scenic Area—great for day trips. A Sno-Park permit is required December 1–April 1. There is good fishing, hunting, biking, mushrooming, berry picking, hiking, and winter sports within a short drive. Trapper Creek Wilderness is within easy walking distance.

FOR MORE INFORMATION
Mt. Adams Ranger District
2455 Hwy 141
Trout Lake, WA 98650
509-395-3400
http://www.fs.fed.us/gpnf/recreation/cabins/index.shtml

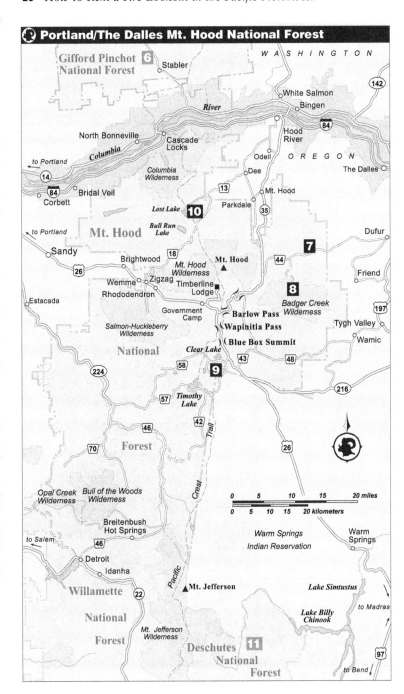

Portland/The Dalles Mt. Hood National Forest

Mt. Hood National Forest

"I am not aware that we ever quarreled."

Henry David Thoreau's response to a pious relative when asked,
on his deathbed, if he had made his peace with God.

7 Fivemile Butte Lookout

YOUR BEARINGS

20 miles west of Dufur

35 miles southeast of the town of Hood River

35 miles southwest of The Dalles

115 miles southeast of Portland via The Dalles and Dufur—though only
70 miles via Highway 26.

AVAILABILITY Available year-round.

CAPACITY Four people maximum, though two would be more comfortable. Not suitable for small children.

DESCRIPTION 14 x 14-foot room with catwalk, atop a 40-foot tower. Storage shed with firewood and outhouse at ground level. Superb views.

Fivemile Butte Lookout

In 2002, Fivemile Lookout received new girding and railing on the stairways. The wood on the catwalk railing was refinished and the shed was re-roofed, painted, and repaired. In 2003, a new wood stove and hearth were put into the Lookout, the floor was re-tiled, and a new door and a new roof were installed. In 2004, new paint, inside and out, and re-glazing of window moldings was scheduled. A solar lighting system has been installed in the cabin. Since Fivemile Lookout is rented year-round, two weeks are reserved during the summer months for these annual repair and maintenance efforts.

COST $30 per night.

RESERVATIONS Call the toll-free National Recreation Reservation Service at 1-877-444-6777 or make reservations online at www.ReserveUSA.com.

Websites: http://www.fs.fed.us/r6/mthood/
http:// www.naturenw.org/cab-hood.htm

SAFETY CONSIDERATIONS During a typical winter it will be necessary to leave your car in a parking area and travel by skis or snowshoes the final three miles to the lookout. Be prepared for extreme weather conditions. Forest Service Roads 44 and 4430 are closed from December 15th through March 15th, from the junction of Forest Service Road 44/4430 to Highway 35. During this time park at Billy Bob Sno-Park. A Northwest Forest Pass is required for this Sno-park. Useful phone numbers: Avalanche Information (503) 808-2400; current weather update (503) 225-5555, ext 6026.

Access by skis for a good to moderately skilled skier takes approximately four hours. The route is marked with orange, arrow-shaped mileage signs. Be prepared for extreme weather conditions. Always contact the Ranger District prior to your departure for the latest road and weather conditions.

Because of the height of the lookout and its open catwalk, it may be risky to bring children. The stairway and catwalk are wooden and are quite slippery in rain, snow, and ice. Occasionally, during strong winds, the tower may sway slightly. It is built to do this. It is safer to remain in the lookout than to attempt to descend the stairway during wind storms or lightning. The lookout is well-grounded. Enjoy the spectacle.

HOW TO GET THERE Travel west on Dufur Valley Road from the town of Dufur for a little over 18 miles to Forest Road 4430, following the sign for ramsey hall and camp baldwin. Dufur Valley Road becomes Dufur Mill Road, and then Forest Road 44. It is paved all the way.

You may park your vehicle here at the junction of Roads 4430 and 44. There are two routes from this point; one is three miles long, the other is four. The two are clearly marked, and together offer an excellent loop route to and from the lookout. (There is additional parking at

Camp Baldwin, about a mile east). To follow the first route, turn right on Forest Road 4430 for about 0.75 mile to Forest Road 120. Turn left onto Road 120, and after 1.5 to 2 miles, take another left onto Road 122, (not shown on map) from where you will see a green gate leading to the lookout.

The alternate route from the junction of Roads 44 and 4430 is less than four miles long, and takes you about two miles west on Road 44 (past its junction with Road 4430) to Road 120. Turn right onto Road 120 and follow this to Road 122 (not shown on map) and the green gate leading to the lookout. If you're lucky enough to be driving, neither Road 120 nor Road 122 is maintained—though they are negotiable, more or less.

Just north of Forest Road 44, on Forest Road 4430, there is a lovely campground set among tall firs, pines, and cedars stretched out languidly along Eight Mile Creek, called Eight Mile Crossing. Unfortunately, on the day we were there, there were trailers and mobile homes back to back and side to side, some of them nearly as big as an entire Irish Village.

ELEVATION 4627 feet

WHAT IS PROVIDED The lookout is immaculately clean and newly refurbished. There is one double bed, propane cook stove and fuel, table and chairs, fire extinguisher, woodstove, firewood, shovel, a few dishes and utensils, and maps of the area. A rope-and-pulley system transports gear up to the catwalk.

The two-way radio is to be used for emergency communications only.

WHAT TO BRING Drinking water is a must, or the means to treat local water. Snow can be melted for your washing needs, but the Forest Service says that safe drinking water from snow cannot be assured. Extra food is a must—severe weather conditions may delay your intended departure. Prepare for harsh weather and pack accordingly.

HISTORY This lookout site was established around 1930. The present cabin was built in the early 1960s. This structure is still used as a fire lookout throughout the summer months.

AROUND YOU Magnificent 360-degree views. To the north is snow-covered Mt. Adams and to the west, just 10 miles away, is Mt. Hood. A new trail now offers hikers access to the lookout from Eight Mile Creek.

This is a shared winter recreation area. You are likely to share the area with snow-mobilers and winter outdoor enthusiasts.

FOR MORE INFORMATION
Barlow Ranger District—Dufur Ranger Station
780 NE Court Street
Dufur, Oregon 97021
(541) 467-2291
http://www.fs.fed.us/r6/mthood/recreation/lookouts/index.shtml

Mid August at Sourdough Mountain Lookout

Down valley a smoke haze
Three days heat, after five days rain
Pitch glows on the fir-cones
Across rocks and meadows
Swarms of new flies.
I cannot remember things I once read
A few friends, but they are in cities.
Drinking cold snow-water from a tin cup
Looking down for miles
Through high still air.

Gary Snyder, *No Nature*

"Heaven parted and we floated gleefully until parting."
From the Lookout's Guestbook

Flag Point Lookout

YOUR BEARINGS

30 miles southwest of Dufur
45 miles southwest of The Dalles
50 miles southeast of the town of Hood River
125 miles southeast of Portland via The Dalles and Dufur—though only
   80 miles via Highway 26

AVAILABILITY November 1 through May 31.

CAPACITY Four people maximum, though two would be more comfortable. Not suitable for small children.

DESCRIPTION A clean and well maintained 14 x 14-foot room atop a 60-foot tower, with splendid views. A rope and pulley system transports gear up to the catwalk.

Flag Point Lookout received new girding and railings on its long stairway up the 60-foot tower. In 2002, a new shed was built adjacent to the Lookout. In 2003, a new wood stove and hearth were installed in the cabin and the floor was re-tiled. The cabin received a new roof as well that year. In 2004, the cabin was repainted inside and out and a new door was mounted. The windows were re-glazed. A solar lighting system has been installed in the cabin. These projects occur during the summer months while the Lookout is in fire duty service.

Flag Point Lookout

COST $30 per night.

RESERVATIONS Call the toll-free National Recreation Reservation Service at 1-877-444-6777 or make reservations online at www.ReserveUSA.com.

SAFETY CONSIDERATIONS Winter access can be moderate to difficult and you should be prepared for extreme weather. During a typical winter it will be necessary to leave your car in a parking area and travel by skis or snowshoes the final 11 miles to the lookout. Access by skis takes a minimum of eight hours and is *not* a trip for novices. Normal winter access to Flag Point begins from the junction of Forest Road 44 and 4430 at the Billy Bob Sno-Park. Forest Service Roads 44 and 4430 are closed from December 15th through March 15th, from the junction of Forest Service Road 44/4430 to Highway 35. During this time park at Billy Bob Sno-Park. A Northwest Forest Pass is required for this Sno-park. Useful phone numbers: Avalanche Information (503) 808-2400; Current Weather Update (503) 225-5555, ext. 6026.

The trail is marked with orange, arrow-shaped mileage signs. Be prepared for extreme weather conditions. You may need to spend a night out en route.

The height of the lookout—60 feet above the ground—as well as its open catwalk, makes this rental risky for children, even with automobile access. Both stairway and catwalk are wooden and are slippery in rain, snow, and ice. Occasionally, during strong winds, the tower will sway slightly. It's built to do this. It is safer to remain in the cabin than to attempt to descend the stairway during wind storms or lightning. The lookout is well grounded. Enjoy nature's fireworks.

HOW TO GET THERE Travel west on Dufur Valley Road from the town of Dufur for a little over 18 miles to Forest Road 4430, following the sign for RAMSEY HALL and CAMP BALDWIN. Dufur Valley Road becomes Dufur Mill Road, and then Forest Road 44. It is paved all the way. The route is clearly signed. Winter access can range from moderate to difficult depending on snow conditions. You may park your vehicle at the junction of Roads 4430 and 44. (There is additional parking at Camp Baldwin, about a mile east).

Follow Forest Road 44 west to its junction with Forest Road 4420—about 1.5miles. Turn left and follow Road 4420 for 2.5 miles—where it becomes Road 2730. Follow Road 2730 for 3.5miles to Road 200: turn right here. The lookout is 3.7 miles ahead—though the sign says three miles.

Please consult the Ranger District regarding current road and snow conditions prior to your departure. All the roads are paved except for Road 200, which is not maintained—though it was navigable the day we drove it.

For those unwilling to go the whole way to the lookout in a single day there is a delectable little campground just beyond halfway, at Fifteen Mile Creek, at the edge of Badger Creek Wilderness. There is space for only three tents here, one of which is on the banks of the creek. The creek is within the Dufur Municipal Watershed so please take good care of it. Fifteen Mile Trail (456) passes through here, and yes, it is 10.3 miles long.

ELEVATION 5650 feet

WHAT IS PROVIDED Propane cook stove and fuel, table and chairs, a single bed, fire extinguisher, firewood, shovel, a few dishes and utensils, and area maps. It has a small sink, a fridge with freezer, and a woodstove. The lookout is equipped with solar panels, and if the gods smile on you, you may have solar light for an hour or so, after dark of course.

Fifty-six steps take you, gasping, to the cabin, though a rope-and-pulley system will transport your gear straight up with blessed ease. An outhouse, and a storage shed containing firewood are on the ground below. The lookout is equipped with a satellite link telephone with instructions and emergency phone numbers posted nearby. This is to be used only for emergency communications, not for ordering pizza.

Like many of the Forest Service rentals, this lookout has a guest-book where visitors may leave something behind for those yet to come.

5-1-95: The sleep on the catwalk was great. Stayed toasty in the bag, and what a sunrise! Now it's back to civilization to pick up Dead tickets. Life is hell. P.S. Many thanks to the Forest Service for this great spot.

3-27-94: Skied in by the light of a perfect full moon. Enjoyed two beautiful days of sunshine, blue skies, good friends and soft spring rain. Hard to imagine a cabin with a better view. Love this place.

12-31-93: We celebrated New Year's Eve with champagne and OPB. Happy New Year, world. The trees danced in the wind outside, we danced inside. Glorious winter storm. Thank you Forest Service staff for making this available.

WHAT TO BRING Drinking water is a must, or the means to treat the local water. Snow can be melted for your washing needs, but the Forest Service says that safe drinking water from snow cannot be assured. Extra food is a must—severe weather conditions may delay your intended departure time.

Prepare for harsh weather and pack accordingly.

HISTORY The original site was established in 1930. The tower and cabin were re-built in the early 1960s. The cabin still serves as a summer home for the fire lookout who plays a key role in the detection of forest fires on the Barlow Ranger District and adjoining lands.

AROUND YOU This fire lookout is unique in that it is the only one we have come across that is surrounded by wilderness. It is approximately 15 miles southeast of Mt. Hood in the North Cascade Mountains, and within Badger Creek Wilderness.

From the lookout you will see Mt. Hood, snow-covered of course, close up and to the west. Mt. Adams, also snow-covered, is to the north. On a clear day one can catch glimpses of Mount St. Helens, and, we're told, even Mt. Rainier. To the south: Mt. Jefferson and the Three Sisters.

Trails beside the lookout: Douglas Cabin Trail (470) takes you south to Sunrise Spring (.5 mile), and Helispot (2.2 miles). About a mile before reaching the lookout there are the following trails off Forest Road 200 which take you into the heart of Badger Creek Wilderness: Badger Creek Cutoff Trail (477), Divide Trail (458), and the Little Badger Trail (469). They are all are open to horses, for better or worse, and there is parking at the trailheads.

This is a shared winter recreation area. You are likely to share the area with snow-mobilers and winter outdoor enthusiasts.

FOR MORE INFORMATION
Barlow Ranger District—Dufur Ranger Station
780 NE Court Street
Dufur, Oregon 97021
(541) 467-2291
http://www.fs.fed.us/r6/mthood/recreation/lookouts/index.shtml

"Love is a call to action."

Kevin Peer, Documentary Filmmaker

Clear Lake Lookout

YOUR BEARINGS
60 miles southeast of Portland
60 miles southwest of The Dalles
50 northwest of Madras

AVAILABILITY November 1 through May 31. This is a winter rental only. The Ranger District began renting this facility on January 15, 2000.

CAPACITY Four people, although one or two would be more comfortable. Not suitable for small children.

DESCRIPTION 14 x 14-foot cabin atop 40-foot tower.

COST $30 per night.

RESERVATIONS Call toll-free the National Recreation Reservation Service at 1-877-444-6777 or make reservations online at www.ReserveUSA.com.

SAFETY CONDITIONS Winter access easy to moderate depending on snow conditions. It takes approximately 3.5 to 4 hours to cross-country ski to the Lookout. The elevation climbs 900 feet. Be prepared for extreme weather conditions. This is a good ski for moderate to experienced skiers. For all Lookout routes you should be experienced in backcountry winter travel and survival skills. Useful phone numbers: Avalanche Information (503) 808-2400; Current Weather Update (503) 225-5555, ext. 6026.

HOW TO GET THERE Normal access begins at the junction of Highway 26 and Forest Service Road 42 at the Skyline Sno-Park. Park at the Sno-park and ski, snowshoe, or snowmobile into the Lookout Tower. The Mt. Hood Snowmobile Club grooms the road to the facility. Proceed on Road 42 to the 240 spur road and on to the Lookout. It is approximately 3.2 miles to the tower from the Sno-park.

You must purchase a Sno-Park Permit to leave your car at Skyline Sno-Park. These can be purchased at several locations in the Portland area, at the Mt. Hood Information Center in Welches, or at CJ's on Highway 26 prior to your arrival.

ELEVATION 4454 feet

WHAT IS PROVIDED Propane stove, single bed, table, chairs, and firewood. You will also find a table and chair, a fire extinguisher, broom, mop, and bucket. There is a limited number of dishes, pots, pans, and utensils, a map of the area, and a shovel. A solar lighting system has been installed in the cabin. On the ground are an outhouse and a shed.

Clear Lake had a new shed built in 2002. A new roof was put on the electrical room and a new refrigerator was added. In 2003 a new wood stove and hearth were installed and a new roof was fitted.

Clear Lake Lookout

In 2004, Clear Lake Lookout had a new toilet built. These projects are all accomplished during the summer months while the facility is in fire duty service.

WHAT TO BRING Drinking water is a must, or the means to treat the local water. Snow can be melted for your washing needs, but the Forest Service says that safe drinking water from snow cannot be assured. Extra food is a must—severe weather conditions may delay your intended departure time. Bring a cell phone in case of an emergency.

Prepare for harsh weather and pack accordingly.

HISTORY The original site was established around 1930. The cabin and tower were re-built in the 1960s. Maintenance continues to occur during the summer fire season.

AROUND YOU This is a shared winter recreation area. You are likely to share the area with snow-mobilers and winter outdoor enthusiasts.

FOR MORE INFORMATION
Barlow Ranger District
780 NE Court
Dufur, OR 97021
(541) 467-2291
http://www.fs.fed.us/r6/mthood/recreation/lookouts/index.shtm

---

"I want to go soon and live away by the pond, where I shall hear only the wind whispering among the reeds. It will be success if I shall have left myself behind."
Henry David Thoreau, *Journal*, December 24, 1841

10 Lost Lake Cabins

YOUR BEARINGS
20 miles west of Hood River Ranger Dist. in Mt. Hood-Parkdale
30 miles southwest of the town of Hood River
50 miles southwest of The Dalles
90 miles southeast of Portland

AVAILABILITY May through October, depending on snow conditions.

CAPACITY A maximum of 15 people in the log cabin and in each of the two Adirondack shelters. However, a group half that size would be more comfortable. Ideal for families.

DESCRIPTION One 15 x 15-foot log cabin, two three-sided Adirondack structures, and one hexagonal, canvas-covered structure. All are very pleasantly situated.

The cabin, which is wheelchair-accessible, consists of a single room with exposed log walls, shingle roof, and a lovely hardwood floor. The cabin also has massive hand-hewn beams overhead, two skylights, a vaulted ceiling, lakeside windows with folding wooden shutters, and a woodstove with a stone chimney. The firewood is stored in a cellar under the house but, ingeniously, can be retrieved by a trap door in the floor beside the stove.

COST Lost Lake Cabins rent at $45 to $100 per night. These structures have a minimum of two nights stay—three on holiday weekends. The entire area—the two Adirondack shelters, the log cabin, and the canvas-covered hexagonal shelter—can be rented for $150 per night during weekends or $100 per night during the week. The structures accommodate a maximum of 45 people. There are parking spaces for 15 vehicles. A two-night deposit is required.

RESERVATIONS These cabins are very popular, requiring reservations well in advance—for the busiest weekends in July and August, as much as 12 months ahead. For information and reservations, contact:

Lost Lake Resort and Campground
P.O. Box 90
Hood River, OR 97031
(541) 386-6366

HOW TO GET THERE From Portland, Oregon, travel east on Interstate 84 to the first Hood River exit (Exit 62). Travel through the town of Hood River on Oak Street to the stoplight at 13th Street. Turn right onto 13th Street and continue through town. After two miles the road name

Lost Lake Cabins

changes to Tucker Road. Stay on Tucker Road for two miles—to the Wind Master Corner intersection. Turn left—still Tucker Road—and continue for two miles to Tucker Bridge. After crossing the bridge veer right (downhill) onto Dee Highway (State 281), and continue south along the West Fork Hood River to the town of Dee. Turn right onto Lost Lake Road, which is Forest Road 13. Continue on this paved but winding road for 15 miles to Forest Road 1340 and the Lost Lake Resort & Campground. Drive through the campground, following the signs for ORGANIZATIONAL CAMPGROUND. The cabins are about one mile beyond the entrance to Lost Lake Resort and Campground.

ELEVATION 3140 feet

WHAT IS PROVIDED There are four single beds—benches, really, affixed to the walls. They do not fold away, but they double as fine seats. Bring a sleeping pad or mattress of some kind—unless you don't mind sleeping on bare wood.

There is a fine hand-hewn picnic table inside also—though no cooking facilities apart from the barbecue and fire ring outside, where there is also a delightful porch with views of the lake.

In the area between the cabin and the Adirondack shelters is a vault toilet, a pleasant saunter away. About 100 yards from the cabin is a hexagonal structure with a canvas roof, and four picnic tables. This can be used by as many as 50 people as a gathering place.

WHAT TO BRING Cooking utensils, and fishing gear. Since you can drive right to the rentals, take anything and everything you need to make your stay comfortable.

THE SETTING In almost every respect these three structures fail to fulfill our criteria for inclusion in this book, for they are neither remote nor secluded, and are adjacent to Lost Lake Resort, which has a store, boat launch (though, mercifully, no motorized boats are allowed) and, on the day we were there, seemed almost as busy as downtown Portland on a Friday afternoon.

Yet we have included these because they are unique. The Lost Lake Cabin was constructed in 1992 from existing Civilian Conservation Corps blueprints that date back to the 1930s. It was built as part of an ongoing series of workshops organized by Mt. Hood National Forest, and taught by experts from all over the country specializing in obscure but lovely trades, such as masonry and blacksmithing. Students and other participants pay tuition and fees of several hundred dollars to learn the myriad of skills involved—everything from log-cabin construction to ornamental-hardware fabrication.

The two Adirondack shelters, three-sided with no front wall, were restored during a series of workshops, and the grand barbecue was built from solid stone by the masons and their students. It is most regrettable that the insides of these lovely structures have been almost completely covered with graffiti. Though structurally sound they are scarcely habitable in their present condition. One hopes after all the work that has gone into them that the Forest Service will be able to find a solution to this dismaying problem.

However, the Lost Lake Cabin, just beyond the Adirondacks, may be what the wise wilderness doctor ordered for the harassed Portland family. It is in immaculate condition, overlooks the lake, and is far enough away from the bustle of the campground and resort to allow a sense of seclusion and solitude. It is wheelchair-accessible. The cabin itself is remarkable in that it was built entirely without the use of electric tools. Even the ironwork was shaped by blacksmiths and their students on the site.

Lost Lake itself is stocked with tens of thousands of rainbow trout. There are also brook and brown trout and a few kokanee. There are several wheelchair-accessible areas for fishing at the lake, as well as a few wheelchair-accessible picnic sites, campsites, and restrooms.

AROUND YOU There are many old-growth trees in the vicinity. The Pacific Crest Trail is two miles to the southwest. It leads into Columbia Wilderness four miles northwest, and into Mt. Hood Wilderness ten miles southeast.

FOR MORE INFORMATION
Lost Lake Resort and Campground
P.O. Box 90
Hood River, OR 97031
(541) 386-6366

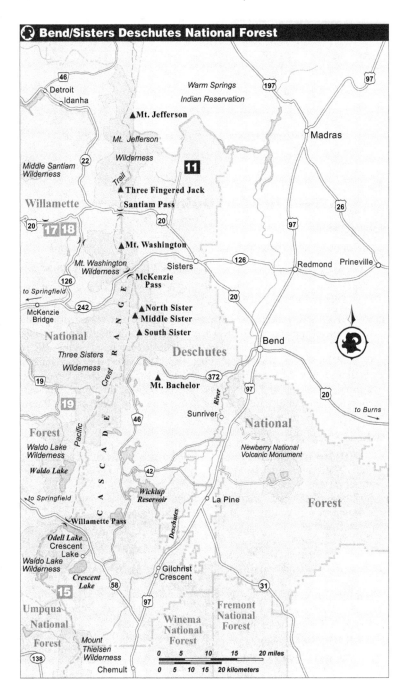

Bend/Sisters Deschutes National Forest

Deschutes National Forest

"Study nature, love nature, stay close to nature. It will never fail you."

Frank Lloyd Wright

11 Green Ridge Lookout

YOUR BEARINGS

23 miles north of Sisters, Oregon

AVAILABILITY April 15 to June 30 and September 15 to November 15

CAPACITY Four people maximum, although two would be more comfortable. Pets are allowed outside only.

DESCRIPTION Green Ridge Lookout sits on the edge of a 16-mile long fault block ridge approximately 500 feet above the Metolius River Valley. The 14 x 14-foot cabin sits on a two-story tower hugging the side of Green Ridge. From the level parking area, there is a short boardwalk to the lower 20 x 20-foot wooden deck—with railings!—from which it is a short, one-story flight of steps to the catwalk of the upper deck surrounding the cabin. Green Ridge is maintained by the Sisters Ranger District as a semi-active fire lookout.

COST $30 per night.

RESERVATIONS Call the toll-free the National Recreation Reservation Service at 1-877-444-6777 or make reservations online at www.ReserveUSA.com. Visit the Deschutes National Forest website for more regional information: http://www.fs.fed.us/r6/centraloregon/. You may reserve your getaway on Green Ridge for as many as seven consecutive nights.

Green Ridge Lookout

HOW TO GET THERE From Sisters, travel 5.5 miles

northwest on US Highway 20 to Forest Service Road 11 at Indian Ford Campground. Turn right on Forest Service Road 11, heading north; travel on the paved road for approximately 10 miles to the end of the pavement and junction of Forest Service Road 1150. Take the left fork, Forest Service Road 1150, to a junction with FSR 1154. Take a left on 1154 to Forest Service Road 1140. Take a left on 1140 to spur road 600. Take a very sharp right on spur road 600 and travel approximately 0.5 mile to a locked gate on the right—spur road 650 (no signs). Unlock the gate with provided key. At the end of the spur road is the Green Ridge Lookout.

Summer access to this tower is possible with any reasonable family vehicle but winter access may require a high-clearance 4x4 vehicle, snowmobile, or cross-county skis, during a season of average snowfall. Check with the Ranger Station before you travel this route in winter.

ELEVATION 4800 feet

WHAT IS PROVIDED Vault toilet, three-burner gas stove/oven, basic cooking and eating utensils, one gas overhead light, propane refrigerator, propane wall heater, one single bed, one table, and two chairs. An outhouse is located at the north end of the parking area.

WHAT TO BRING Food, camping gear, personal gear, adequate clothing protection for severe weather conditions, and garbage bags to remove trash upon leaving. There is no water at the lookout. Bring enough for drinking, cooking, washing, and cleanup for the length of your stay.

HISTORY The lookout was built in 1963 at this site because of its spectacular view of the Metolius River Valley and Mt. Jefferson. It was used for 40 years as a seasonal fire lookout and recently has been occupied by Forest Service volunteers during fire season.

AROUND YOU Picnic on deck below lookout cabin and enjoy the outstanding views of the Metolius River Valley.

FOR MORE INFORMATION
Sisters Ranger District
P.O. Box 249
Sisters, OR 97759
(541) 549-7700
http://www.fs.fed.us/r6/centraloregon/recreation/rentals/index.shtml
http://www.naturenw.org/cab-deschutes.htm

A light exists in spring

A light exists in spring
>Not present on the year
At any other period.
>When March is scarcely here

A color stands abroad
>On solitary hills
That science cannot overtake,
>But human nature feels.

It waits upon the lawn;
>It shows the furthest tree
Upon the furthest slope we know;
>It almost speaks to me.

Then, as horizons step,
>Or noons report away,
Without the formula of sound,
>It passes, and we stay:

A quality of loss
>Affecting our content,
As trade had suddenly encroached
>Upon a sacrament.

Emily Dickinson

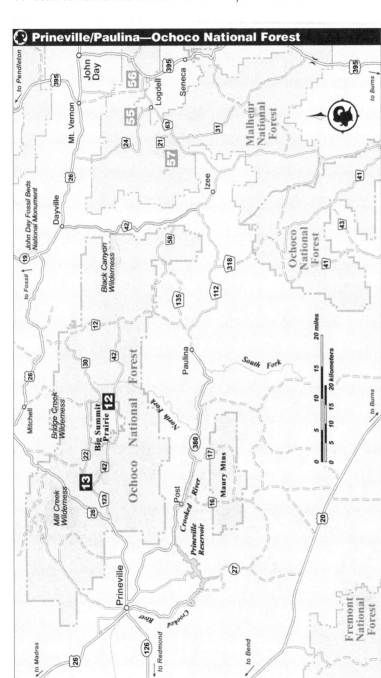

Ochoco National Forest

"To me a lush carpet of pine needles or spongy grass is more welcome than the most luxurious Persian rug."

Helen Keller

12 Cold Springs Guard Station

YOUR BEARINGS

45 miles east of Prineville, Oregon

AVAILABILITY This cabin is available late May to mid-October.

CAPACITY Cabin will sleep six to eight people.

DESCRIPTION An historic cabin near Big Summit Prairie with easy access and many of the amenities of home, including three bedrooms, living room, kitchen, and two bathrooms.

COST $50 per night.

Cold Springs Guard Station

RESERVATIONS Reservations must be made at least four days in advance. The Ochoco National Forest has implemented the National Recreation Reservation System (online reservations) for the Cold Springs Guard Station Rental. You will be able to check for available rental dates or place a reservation for the Cold Springs Cabin using the National Recreation Reservation System website (NRRS). This system will allow you to place your reservation and arrange for payment online using a credit card or money order. There is a fee for each reservation made. Call toll-free 1-877-444-6777 or make reservations online at www.ReserveUSA.com. Check out time is 12:00 P.M. The cabin is available for occupancy at 1:00 P.M. Visit the Ochoco National Forest website for more regional information: http://www.fs.fed.us/r6/centraloregon/.

HOW TO GET THERE To reach Cold Springs, travel 15 miles east from Prineville on Highway 26. Turn right at the junction to the Ochoco Ranger Station on County Road 123 and travel nine miles to the junction of Forest Service Roads 22 and 42. Stay right on Forest Service Road 42 and proceed approximately 22 miles. Just after crossing the North Fork of the Crooked River, turn left on Forest Service Road 30 and proceed approximately 1.5 miles. Signs to Cold Springs will be visible. Turn right at the sign to Cold Springs G.S.

ELEVATION 4620 feet

WHAT IS PROVIDED The rustic cabin is equipped with two bathrooms, one with shower, kitchen, living room, and three bedrooms. Sleeping accommodations include six twin beds and a futon. Drinking water is available in the building. You will enjoy a solar refrigerator, solar and propane lights, propane hot water heater, and propane heat. Propane gas, basic kitchen utensils, cleaning supplies, and some furniture are provided.

WHAT TO BRING You will need to bring food, trash bags, personal gear, and sleeping bags. From Cold Springs, the nearest store and gas station are in Prineville or Mitchell (45 miles away).

HISTORY Generations of firefighters have stayed at the Cold Springs Guard Station, which is set among old-growth ponderosa pine stands and sagebrush meadows. It served a special role as a switchboard station connecting phone calls between the towns of Prineville and Paulina, as well as various fire lookouts and guard stations throughout the region.

The magnetic phone lines were replaced by radio communication during the 1960s. No communication is available at Cold Springs Cabin today, unless you bring your cell phone with you. The cabin you are renting is an historic site. Some of the items here, such as the map of Cold Springs, are left for your enjoyment. Please treat them with care; they are old and fragile.

This station was constructed in 1934 and replaced the original cabin which was damaged by fire. Forest Service crews occupied the dwelling into the 1990s. During the early years, Cold Springs Guard Station was home to the Fire Guard and his family during the summer fire season.

AROUND YOU Old growth ponderosa pines and sagebrush meadows are unique to this site. The diverse habitat provides a home for a variety of wildlife including antelope, deer, elk, geese, and Sandhill cranes. In late spring and early summer, the prairie and surrounding forest are resplendent with wildflowers. Enjoy hiking, mountain biking, and fishing in the vicinity of the cabin.

FOR MORE INFORMATION
Big Summit Ranger District
33700 NE Ochoco RS Road
Prineville, OR 97754
(541) 416-6645
http://www.fs.fed.us/r6/centraloregon/recreation/rentals/index.shtml

"It is a wholesome and necessary thing for us to turn again to the earth and in the contemplation of her beauties to know of wonder and humility."

Rachel Carson

13 Lookout Mountain Bunkhouses

YOUR BEARINGS
25 miles east of Prineville, Oregon

AVAILABILITY From mid-November through March.

CAPACITY Maximum occupancy for each building is eight people. No pets please.

DESCRIPTION Two bunkhouse facilities are available for winter rental. During the summer, these barracks-style buildings serve as living quarters for the Ochoco National Forest seasonal workforce. The cabins, aptly named "Lookout" and "Canyon" are clean, warm, and loaded with amenities. Outside your door find several thousand acres of pine forest, mountain streams, and habitat for countless varieties of wildlife.

COST $60 per night.

RESERVATIONS Call the toll-free the National Recreation Reservation Service at 1-877-444-6777 or make reservations online at www.ReserveUSA.com. Check-in time is 2:00 P.M. and checkout time is

12:00 P.M. Visit the Ochoco National Forest website for more regional information: http://www.fs.fed.us/r6/centraloregon/.

HOW TO GET THERE   To reach the bunkhouse rentals, travel 15 miles east from Prineville on Highway 26. Turn right at the junction to Ochoco Ranger Station on County Road 123 and continue 9 miles to the junction of Forest Roads 22 and 42. The cabins are situated just to the right of this intersection.

ELEVATION   4000 feet

WHAT IS PROVIDED   The bunkhouses are equipped with two bathrooms with showers, kitchen, bedrooms, and a small living room. Both buildings have electricity, electric heat, woodstove, appliances, and hot/cold running water. Basic kitchen utensils, cleaning supplies, beds, and some furniture are provided. Each bunkhouse has small, enclosed bedrooms with a total of five to six beds per bunkhouse. Firewood is provided for the woodstoves.

WHAT TO BRING   Food, trash bags, personal gear, and sleeping bags. The nearest store or gas station is in Prineville, 25 miles away.

HISTORY   The bunkhouses are located at the former Civilian Conservation Corps site known as Camp Mill Creek. The barracks-style dwellings are home to Forest Service summer employees and are therefore available to rent only during the winter months.

AROUND YOU   Walton Sno-Park, located approximately 9 miles from the bunkhouses on Forest Service Road 22, offers a variety of winter activ-

Lookout Mountain Bunkhouses

ities. Cross-country ski trails are available to match every skill level. Scenic loop trails offer an easy workout or a full day of Nordic skiing. The Sno-Park provides access to numerous snowmobile trails including Indian Prairie, Pisgah Mountain, and Scotts Camp Loop. The Round Mountain trail is accessible from both Walton Sno-Park and Lookout Mountain parking areas.

Lookout Mountain Parking Area, on the summit of Forest Service Road 42, offers access to the Lookout Mountain Roadless Area. Note that the road is not plowed on a consistent basis. The trail system is open for both snowmobilers and cross-country skiers. Diamond markers along trail 808 (blue—cross-country skier) and 808A (orange—snowmobile) lead you to the log snow shelter atop the mountain.

Be aware that winter road and weather conditions are always changing and keep safety in mind while enjoying your National Forest.

FOR MORE INFORMATION
Ochoco National Forest
3160 NE 3rd Street
Prineville, OR 97754
(541) 416-6500
http://www.fs.fed.us/r6/centraloregon/recreation/rentals/index.shtml

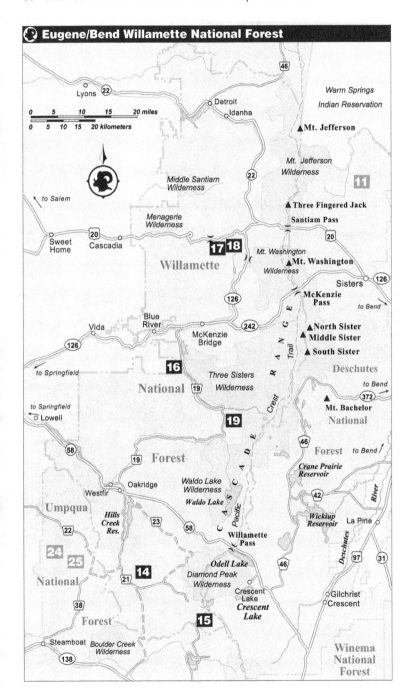

Eugene/Bend Willamette National Forest

Willamette National Forest

❧

"I never found the companion that was so companionable as solitude."

Henry David Thoreau, *Walden*

14 Warner Mountain Lookout

YOUR BEARINGS

35 miles southeast of Oakridge
75 miles southeast of Eugene
140 miles southeast of Salem
140 miles southwest of Bend
190 miles southeast of Portland

AVAILABILITY Mid-November through early May.

CAPACITY Four people maximum; two would be more comfortable. Not suitable for small children. No pets.

DESCRIPTION 14 x 14-foot room atop a 41-foot tower. 6 x 6-foot glassed-in observation cupola. 12 x 14-foot log cabin at ground level. Modern, with panoramic views. A perfect perch for winter weather watching.

COST $40 per night plus $9 reservation fee.

RESERVATIONS The National Recreation Reservation Service (1-877-444-6777 or online at www.ReserveUSA.com). Minimum stay of two nights; maximum stay of seven nights. Check in at 1:00 P.M.; check out at noon.

SAFETY CONSIDERATIONS Always be well-prepared when enter-

Warner Mountain Lookout

ing the backcountry, especially on Warner Mountain in the wintertime. Carry tire chains and a shovel. The lookout is available as a winter rental only. During a typical winter you may be traveling across snow for 6 to 10 miles on skis or snowshoes to reach this remote and spectacular destination. The trip can be extremely difficult in snow and could take an entire day. Plan accordingly, and start early.

This ain't for the faint-hearted. Winter access offers an exciting challenge depending on snow conditions and your condition. The snowline can vary from 2800 feet to 4400 feet. This could mean a total vertical climb on skis or snowshoes of 1400 to 3000 feet. The final two miles are marked with orange poles to guide you across the upper meadows to the lookout. Consult the District Office regarding current road and snow conditions prior to your departure.

Because of the height of the lookout tower and the open catwalk, it might be risky to bring young children. Pets are not allowed. The stairway and catwalk are wooden and become slippery in rain, snow, and ice. Occasionally, during strong winds, the tower will sway slightly. Don't worry, it's built to do this. The Forest Service advises that it is safer to remain in the tower than to attempt to descend the stairway during lightning or a wind storm. The lookout is well grounded.

HOW TO GET THERE From Oakridge, Oregon, travel three miles east on Highway 58. Turn right at Kitson Spring Road, toward Hills Creek Reservoir. After a few hundred yards, veer right onto Forest Road 21 (also called Rigdon Road). Remain on Road 21 as it crosses Hills Creek Reservoir at its southern end. From this point you are traveling a section of the historic Oregon Central Military Wagon Road. There is a 25-mile hiking trail along the banks of the Middle Fork of the Willamette River, which Forest Road 21 parallels. It passes through old-growth stands of Douglas fir, and alongside several campgrounds.

Continue south on Road 21 to its intersection with Forest Road 2129, or until you can drive no further due to snow. There is a small road sign on the right just before Road 2129 but it's easy to miss—at least it was for us. The sign at Road 2129 reads: LOGGERS BUTTE 14, MOON POINT TRAIL 10, but makes nary a mention of the lookout, though all along the way you will have noticed little lookout signs along the road every few miles.

Turn left onto Road 2129, also called Youngs Creek Road, and continue on its gravel surface until immediately after the 8 mile marker, where you reach Forest Road 439. Turn right here. After four miles you see another of those little lookout signs. Turn left; the lookout is less than 0.5 mile away.

ELEVATION 5800 feet

WHAT IS PROVIDED Propane heat, propane oven, and propane light. Fuel is provided. Also a table and chairs, a single bed, fire extinguisher, shovel, and maps of the area. There is a two-way radio available for emergency communications only. An outhouse is several hundred feet down the access road from the lookout.

This is a thoroughly modernized lookout, and should satisfy the whims of even the most thoroughly urbanized. It has fitted carpet, built-in fridge, stove with oven, built-in closets and shelving, built-in double bed, fly-screened windows, even a wood-framed screen door. The windows incidentally, are the modern, metal-framed, sliding type—a departure surely from the original design, though an understandable one.

On the ground there is a lovely log cabin with a shingle roof and, we're sorry to say, a concrete floor. It is available for storage. Even the vault toilet is of log construction, and has a shingle roof.

WHAT TO BRING Drinking water is a must; or the means to treat snowmelt. Snow can be melted for your washing needs, but the Forest Service says that safe drinking water from snow cannot be assured. Extra food is a must—severe weather conditions may delay your departure. Prepare for harsh weather and pack accordingly.

HISTORY This fire lookout was moved here to Warner Mountain from Grass Mountain. The cabin is a newly built replica of the old cupola-style lookout. The prototype for this style was constructed atop Mt. Hood in 1915. The cabin and cupola have 360-degree views.

Warner Mountain Lookout continues to serve as a summer home and duty station for the seasonal fire guards who play a key role in the detection of fires on the Rigdon Ranger District and adjoining forests.

AROUND YOU To the south: Mt. Thielsen, Mt. Scott, and Mt. Bailey. To the northeast: the South and Middle Sisters of the Three Sisters, Broken Top, and Mt. Bachelor. To the east: Diamond Peak and Diamond Peak Wilderness. To the northwest: Hills Creek Reservoir.

Moon Point Trail (3688) is well signed and can be reached from Forest Road 2129 or 439.

FOR MORE INFORMATION
Middle Fork Ranger District
46375 Highway 58
Westfir, Oregon 97492
(541) 782-2283
www.fs.fed.us/r6/willamette/recreation/cabinrentals

"There's no water here but plenty of opportunity for reflection."

Thomas Doty, *Journal*, October 28, 1995

15 Timpanogas Shelter

YOUR BEARINGS

85 miles southeast of Eugene, Oregon

AVAILABILITY Mid-July through the end of October.

CAPACITY The cabin accommodates six to eight people. There is room for camping near the cabin. A maximum of twenty people can be on the site at one time.

DESCRIPTION The log structure measures 15 by 18 feet. It has a sleeping loft. As the cabin is located on Timpanogas Lake, the mosquitoes are prevalent until about mid-August—a month or so after snow melt—so come prepared.

COST $40 per night plus $9 reservation fee.

RESERVATIONS The National Recreation Reservation Service (1-877-444-6777 or online at www.ReserveUSA.com). Minimum stay of two nights; maximum stay of seven nights. Check in at 1:00 P.M.; check out at noon.

Timpanogas Shelter

HOW TO GET THERE From Eugene, Oregon, travel on Highway 58 past the town of Oakridge to Road 21. Continue on Road 21 to Road 2154. Follow Road 2154 for 10 miles (8 of which are gravel surfaced) to Timpanogas Shelter.

ELEVATION 5300 feet

WHAT IS PROVIDED A table and wood stove, as well as an outdoor fire ring are provided.

WHAT TO BRING Water and all personal belongings.

AROUND YOU Fishermen enjoy fishing both upper and lower Timpanogas Lakes—which, by the way, are closed to motor craft. Hikers will enjoy the twenty-plus miles of trails in the Timpanogas area.

FOR MORE INFORMATION
Middle Fork Ranger District
46375 Highway 58
Westfir, Oregon 97492
(541) 782-2283
www.fs.fed.us/r6/willamette/recreation/cabinrentals

"In the sun that is young once only,
Time let me play and be golden in the mercy of his means."
Dylan Thomas, *Fern Hill*

16 Indian Ridge Lookout

YOUR BEARINGS
60 miles northeast of Oakridge
70 miles east of Eugene via Highway 126
95 miles east of Eugene via Highway 58 and Aufderheide Drive
100 miles west of Bend
135 miles southeast of Salem
185 miles southeast of Portland

AVAILABILITY The usual season is from July 1 until September 30, depending snowfall. It is not available for rental during the winter months.

CAPACITY One or two people—maximum of four. Not suitable for small children. No pets.

DESCRIPTION 16 x 16-foot room, all wood and windows, atop a 30-foot tower.

COST $40 per night plus $9 reservation fee.

RESERVATIONS The National Recreation Reservation Service (1-877-444-6777 or online at www.ReserveUSA.com). Reservations may be made for up to three consecutive nights on a first-come–first-served basis—one visit per year. Check in at 2:00 P.M.; check out at 1:00 P.M.

SAFETY CONSIDERATIONS Because of the height of the lookout tower, the open catwalk, and the location, it might be risky to bring young children. From the rocks around the lookout there are concealed vertical drops of a hundred feet or more and there are no guard rails. The stairway and catwalk are wooden and become slippery in rain, snow and ice, and there is no heat.

Occasionally, during strong winds, the tower will sway slightly. Don't worry, it's built to do this. The Forest Service advises that it is safer to remain in the tower than to attempt to descend the stairway during lightning or a wind storm. The lookout is well grounded.

HOW TO GET THERE There are two routes from Eugene, one somewhat longer than the other, though we suggest the longer one because it will take you from south to north along the Robert Aufderheide Memorial Drive—and it is a memorable drive.

To take the Aufderheide route: from Eugene, travel 36 miles southeast on Highway 58 to the Westfir Junction. Turn left here and after two miles you will be at the start of Forest Road 19, the Aufderheide Drive.

Just before you reach the Aufderheide Drive—the Aufderheide National Scenic Byway, to unfurl its complete title—you may notice a red covered bridge over the river. This is known as the Office Bridge. It is, in fact, the longest covered bridge in Oregon, and it is unique in that it has a covered footwalk beside, but separate from, the road-way of the bridge itself.

Indian Ridge Lookout

Back when Willamette National Forest had the reputation of cutting more timber than any other national forest in the country, this section of road was the roadbed for the railroad line that was used to haul millions of trees out of the forest to the mill at Westfir. The tracks were replaced by this road after World War II.

Still on Road 19, you are now traveling parallel to the North Fork of the Middle Fork Willamette River. This is a long and lovely drive, green and watery, shadowed in places by old-growth trees, particularly at Constitution Grove, 27 miles north of Westfir Junction. A short trail takes you through the grove.

Continuing north and east through the Box Canyon area you will travel, first, parallel to Roaring River and, after that, the South Fork of the McKenzie River.

It is about 50 languid miles north from Westfir to Forest Road 1980. Turn left (northwest) here. Follow Road 1980 for 7.3 steep and winding miles of gravel until you reach signed Forest Road 247. Turn right. Continue for another 2.7 miles: there, on the left, you will see a locked green gate and a ROAD CLOSED sign. The lookout is less than 0.25 mile beyond the gate, although you can't see it until you get much closer.

The shorter route, for the brisk, brusque, or just plain busy, is to travel 45 miles east of Eugene on Highway 126 to Forest Road 19, three miles east of Blue River, and turn right. This is the northern end of the Aufderheide Drive. Continue south for 16 miles to Forest Road 1980, which will be on your right, just after French Pete Campground.

Turn right (northwest) onto Road 1980 for 7.3 steep and winding miles of gravel, until you reach Forest Road 247. It is signed. Turn right and continue for another 2.7 miles: there on your left you will see a locked green gate and a ROAD CLOSED sign. The lookout is less than a quarter of a mile beyond the gate, though you can't see it until you get much closer.

Forest Road 247 is quite narrow with precipitous, unguarded cliffs. Drive only in daylight, and very soberly.

ELEVATION 5405 feet

WHAT IS PROVIDED Two nice beds, a table, two chairs, a small chest of drawers, and some shelves. Unfortunately, it has no stove, no sink, no fridge, no heating, no fireplace, no light, and no water, but lots of firewood (for campfires), and an outhouse 50 feet from the Lookout.

The day we were there, in July, there was a family very happily stoking up their own Hibachi on the rocks beside the tower.

WHAT TO BRING Water. While most lookouts do not have inside potable water, this is the only one we have come across in our travels that is rented so bereft of what many would consider the basic essentials. If you are renting in early spring or late fall, good sleeping bags are a must, as are warm clothing and, of course, some form of lighting, heating, and cooking equipment.

HISTORY Built in 1958, it is still used intermittently for fire detection during the summer months.

AROUND YOU Three Sisters and Mt. Bachelor are to the east. Diamond Peak is to the south. Mt. Jefferson, Three Fingered Jack and Sand Mountain are to the northeast Mt. Hood and Mt. Washington are to the north, and the foothills of the Cascades are seen to the west.

Beneath you, off a sheer drop of several hundred feet, is a perfectly circular pond surrounded by tall trees.

Marring the spectacular view, somewhat, are three eyesores in the shape of three antennae that look like they were dropped there by angry aliens who had been refused Green Cards.

FOR MORE INFORMATION
McKenzie River Ranger District
57600 McKenzie Hwy
McKenzie Bridge, OR 97413
(541) 822-3381
www.fs.fed.us/r6/willamette/recreation/cabinrentals

"The strongest and sweetest songs are yet to be sung."
Walt Whitman, "Boughs"

17 Fish Lake Remount Depot Commissary Cabin

YOUR BEARINGS
22 miles northeast of McKenzie Bridge

AVAILABILITY Fridays through Mondays from Thanksgiving Weekend to mid-March.

CAPACITY Four people maximum; no pets allowed.

DESCRIPTION A rustic two-room cabin.

COST $40 per night plus $9 reservation fee.

RESERVATIONS The National Recreation Reservation Service (1-877-444-6777 or online at www.ReserveUSA.com). Minimum stay of two nights; maximum stay of three nights. Check in at 11:00 A.M.; check out at 1:00 P.M.. This rental is limited to a single reservation per group per season.

HOW TO GET THERE   Travel to the junction of Highway 126 and Highway 20. The access road is not plowed in winter so renters may need to ski or snowshoe the 0.75 mile into the cabin on an existing trail.

ELEVATION   3200 feet

WHAT TO BRING   Sleeping bags, food, water, warm clothing, personal items and winter safety items. Be prepared to pack out your own garbage.

WHAT IS PROVIDED   Propane heating and cooking stoves, solar-powered lighting, table and chairs, basic kitchen utensils, full size bed, and a sofa. An outhouse is located outside the cabin.

HISTORY   The Commissary Cabin was built in 1924, along with the other cabins and associated structures on this site that remain today. These include a dispatcher's cabin, Hall House cabin, a springhouse shed, a garage and woodshed and a fire hose shelter.

AROUND YOU   Marked Nordic ski trails and snowmobile trails are found at the nearby Lava Lake Sno-Park. Within a 15-minute drive of the area you will find seven Sno-parks constituting the Santiam Pass Winter Recreation Area.

FOR MORE INFORMATION
McKenzie River Ranger District
57600 McKenzie Hwy
McKenzie Bridge, OR 97413
(541) 822-3381
www.fs.fed.us/r6/willamette/recreation/cabinrentals

Fish Lake Remount Depot Commissary Cabin

> *"When we try to pick out anything by itself we find it hitched to everything else in the universe."*
>
> John Muir

18 Fish Lake Remount Depot Hall House

YOUR BEARINGS
22 miles northeast of McKenzie Bridge.

AVAILABILITY Fridays through Mondays from Thanksgiving weekend to mid-March.

CAPACITY Four people maximum; no pets allowed.

DESCRIPTION Hall House, the original Supervisor's cabin, contains three rooms.

COST $60 per night plus $9 reservation fee.

RESERVATIONS The National Recreation Reservation Service (1-877-444-6777 or online at www.ReserveUSA.com). Minimum stay of two nights; maximum stay of three nights. Check in at 11:00 A.M.; check out at 1:00 P.M.. This rental is limited to a single reservation per group per season.

HOW TO GET THERE Travel to the junction of Highway 126 and Highway 20. The access road is not plowed in winter so renters may need to ski or snowshoe the 0.75 mile into the cabin on an existing trail.

ELEVATION 3200 feet

WHAT IS PROVIDED Propane heating and cooking stoves, solar-powered lighting, table and chairs, basic kitchen utensils, full size bed and a sofa. An outhouse is located outside the cabin.

WHAT TO BRING Sleeping bags, food, water, warm clothing, personal items and winter safety items. Be prepared to pack out your own garbage.

HISTORY Hall House was built in 1924, along with the other cabins and associated structures on this site that remain today. These

Fish Lake Remount Depot Hall House

include a dispatcher's cabin, Commissary Cabin, a springhouse shed, a garage and woodshed and a fire hose shelter.

AROUND YOU Marked Nordic ski trails and snowmobile trails are found at the nearby Lava Lake Sno-Park. Within a 15-minute drive of the area you will find seven Sno-parks constituting the Santiam Pass Winter Recreation Area.

FOR MORE INFORMATION
McKenzie River Ranger District
57600 McKenzie Hwy
McKenzie Bridge, OR 97413
(541)822-3381
www.fs.fed.us/r6/willamette/recreation/cabinrentals

"Our deepest fear is not that we are inadequate,
our deepest fear is that we are powerful beyond measure."
Nelson Mandela, 1994 Inaugural Address

19 Box Canyon Guard Station

YOUR BEARINGS
35 miles northeast of Oakridge
75 miles southeast of Eugene
105 miles west of Bend
135 miles southeast of Salem
185 miles southeast of Portland

AVAILABILITY Mid-June through September 30, depending on snow levels. It is not available to rent during the winter months.

CAPACITY Up to six people, but two adults, with perhaps one or two small children, would be much more comfortable.

DESCRIPTION 21 x 15-foot, two-room log cabin, in need of some T.L.C.

COST $40 per night plus $9 reservation fee.

RESERVATIONS The National Recreation Reservation Service (1-877-444-6777 or online at www.ReserveUSA.com). Reservations can be made for up to seven consecutive nights on a first-come, first-served basis, with a minimum stay of two nights. Check in at 2:00 P.M.; check out at 1:00 P.M.

HOW TO GET THERE Travel 45 miles east from Eugene on Highway 126, to Forest Road 19—which is five miles east of the Blue River Ranger District. Turn right onto Road 19. This becomes the Robert Aufderheide Memorial Drive. Continue south for about 26 miles. It is paved all the way. The guard station is across the road from Box Canyon Horse Camp.

Another route, and the one we recommend, is to travel 36 miles east of Eugene on Highway 58 to the Westfir Junction. Turn left here and in two miles you will be at the beginning of Forest Road 19, the Robert Aufderheide Memorial Drive. Box Canyon Guard Station is 33 miles from Highway 58 on Road 19.

The Aufderheide Drive, named for a former Supervisor of the Willamette National Forest, is one of the leafiest, greenest, shadiest, quietest, loveliest, wateriest drives you are likely to find. It follows the Wild and Scenic North Fork of the Middle Fork Willamette River most of the way to Box Canyon. We took this route in late July and saw fewer than a half-dozen cars the entire trip.

Box Canyon Guard Station is on the right, as you drive north, just past the sign for Skookum Creek Campground.

ELEVATION 3620 feet

WHAT IS PROVIDED The kitchen/living room has a sink, faucets (not drinking water), a fold-out couch, woodstove, a two-burner-counter-top propane cook stove, closets, cupboards, chairs, and a table that has seen better days. There are no lights and no fridge. Firewood is provided.

The bedroom has two wooden single beds, and a separate entrance. There is an attached woodshed stocked with firewood for your use at the rear of the building. Some of the windows are fly-screened: all have shutters and curtains.

The cabin sits in a nicely fenced yard. There is a vault toilet, a picnic table, a fire ring and a round horse-corral, about 45 feet in diameter. You are welcome to use it, even for the kids. There is a Horse Camp across the road as well, built by the Civilian Conservation Corps in 1933. We were practically whinnying ourselves when we left.

Box Canyon Guard Station

WHAT TO BRING All the water you need, or have the means to treat the local supply, since the water in the cabin is not potable, and in any event, is turned off at the onset of the first frost.

HISTORY Box Canyon was named in 1880 by Charles McClane and Major Sears for its boxy shape. In 1934 the Forest Service built the guard station here to house a fire guard.

AROUND YOU Beside the cabin, in the yard, is the trailhead for the McBee Trail (3523), which takes you into the Three Sisters Wilderness, 5.2 miles away. It also leads to the Crossing Way Trail (3307), 4.7 miles away, which in turn leads north to Roaring River Ridge or south to Three Sisters Wilderness. The Elk Creek Trail (3510), 9.5 miles away, can also be reached via the McBee Trail. Other wilderness trailheads can be found at Skookum Campground a few miles south at the end of Forest Road 1957. Across the road from the cabin in the Box Canyon Horse Camp is the trailhead for the Grasshopper Trail (3306). This leads to Chucksney Mountain, an area that the Forest Service calls, in lovely bureaucratese, "an undeveloped roadless recreation area."

There is a sign nearby on the road that has an interesting message:

Spotted Owls

The forest west of this point is managed for four pair of northern spotted owls who prefer old growth timber. The Forest Service has therefore protected some old growth habitat for the spotted owls. Within these areas, man's activities are restricted to reduce the impact on the foraging range and nesting areas of these birds.

A few hundred yards north on Forest Road 19, on the same side of the road as Box Canyon Guard Station, is Landess Cabin, set in a lovely meadow. This is a replica, built in 1972 by the Forest Service and a neighborhood youth corps, of the original cabin, which was built in 1918 by G. J. Landess and Smith Taylor for a Forest Service Fire Guard. It is not habitable.

About two miles south on Forest Road 19 is the trailhead for Trail 3567, which enters Waldo Lake Wilderness—less than 0.5 mile from the trailhead.

FOR MORE INFORMATION
McKenzie River Ranger District
57600 McKenzie Hwy
McKenzie Bridge, OR 97413
(541) 822-3381
www.fs.fed.us/r6/willamette/recreation/cabinrentals

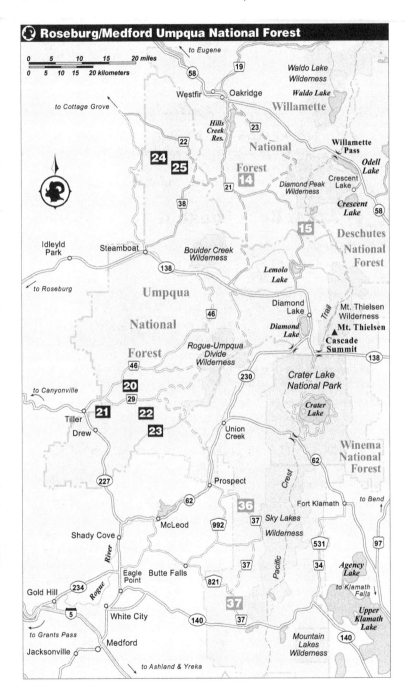

Roseburg/Medford Umpqua National Forest

Umpqua National Forest

"It isn't only the fact that you're alone, but the height and the amount of country you see makes it like being suspended between heaven and earth."

Martha Hardy, Lookout Guard, 1945

20 Acker Rock Lookout

YOUR BEARINGS

30 miles northeast of Tiller
60 miles east Canyonville
80 miles south of Roseburg
150 miles south of Eugene

AVAILABILITY As of this printing, Acker Rock Lookout is temporarily withdrawn from the recreation rental system for the purpose of major renovation work. A completion date is unknown at this time. Please contact the Tiller Ranger Stations for updates. It will return to the rental program once restoration is complete.

CAPACITY The lookout is designed to accommodate four people maximum, although for comfort we recommend no more than two. Not suitable for small children.

DESCRIPTION 12 x 12-foot cabin with narrow catwalk, perched high on a cliff. Spectacular views.

COST $40 per night.

RESERVATIONS The National Recreation Reservation Service (1-877-444-6777 or online at www.ReserveUSA.com).

When you visit Tiller Ranger Station to pick up your keys, we suggest you take the short trail to historic Red Mountain Lookout—relocated piece by piece to a small knoll on the grounds. Originally constructed in 1928 atop Red Mountain, this lookout is a fine example of the cupola-style design common in the 1930s. It was moved here in the autumn of 1985. It is not for rent.

HOW TO GET THERE From Tiller, Oregon, travel northeast on County Road 46 along the South Fork Umpqua River. This road parallels the river for 6.5 miles, where it becomes Forest Road 28, at the Forest boundary.

You will be traveling a two-lane paved road through a lush forested canyon, leaving the broad Umpqua Valley behind. Along the way there are several campgrounds with access to the river, as well as waterfalls, hiking trails, and swimming holes.

Travel on Forest Road 28 for 12.2 miles. Turn right onto Forest Road 29 over a bridge across the South Umpqua River. At this point the road becomes a single-lane road with turnouts. Wonderful views of Acker Rock await you on the approach.

After 5.7 miles on Road 29, turn left onto Forest Road 2838, the turnoff for Acker Rock. This is a single-lane gravel road. After 1.6 miles turn left onto the 950 spur road, which is often gated and locked. Check with the Ranger Station to make sure you'll have clear access to the trailhead.

Unlock the gate and travel one mile on a steep, narrow road to the Acker Rock trailhead. The Acker Rock Trail (1585) is a half-mile, moderate-to-steep hike up to the lookout.

The trail cuts steeply through virgin Douglas fir forest. At the knife-edge ridgetop, climb the 27 wooden steps to the cabin's door. The fencing on the final stretch allows you to look ahead without worrying about your footing. Before the fence was built, all that existed on the precarious summit to guide your final access was a wire cable.

ELEVATION 4112 feet

WHAT IS PROVIDED Propane cook stove and fuel, lights and fridge, wood-stove, single bed, table, and chairs. An open-air pit toilet is nearby among the trees.

WHAT TO BRING Drinking water is a must: it is not provided, though there is a spigot with potable water at the Tiller Ranger Station.

SETTING This lookout cabin anchored atop Acker Rock offers an expansive view of the upper South Umpqua watershed. The rock formation on which the lookout building sits is

Acker Rock Lookout

magnificent; sheer cliffs drop off for several hundred feet on the west and south sides.

Perched on an andesite cliff 2000 feet above the valley floor, you must be half mountain goat to relish this place. If you are queasy at heights, we recommend you choose a different rental. For those who think like a cloud, this is your spot.

The structure is creaky and weather beaten, but solid. A narrow cat-walk around the lookout offers views of a patchwork of timber-producing landscapes including reforested clearcuts old and new. The foreground is dominated by rocks, trees and mountain air. The immediate area offers many large "thinking rocks" that are suspended over the valley—places to ponder gravity, to ponder balance.

The open-air pit toilet has views of sky and branches waving in the wind. We noticed a knotted pull rope leading up to it, via a steep but short trail. If you got this far, you probably won't need it.

HISTORY Before the advent of airplane surveillance for fire detection, more than a dozen lookouts guarded the forests of the Tiller Ranger District. Acker Rock Lookout and Pickett Butte Lookout are the only ones that remain. Pickett Butte is available for rent also.

AROUND YOU Panoramic view of landmarks along the Rogue-Umpqua Divide and magnificent peaks in the Rogue basin. On a clear day you can see the mountains in the Willamette, Rogue and Deschutes River watersheds. Several trails are maintained in the Tiller Ranger District for you to enjoy during your stay.

FOR MORE INFORMATION
Umpqua National Forest
Tiller Ranger Station
27812 Tiller Trail Hwy
Tiller, OR 97484
(541) 825-3100
http://www.fs.fed.us/r6/umpqua/rec/bldg_rnt/rec_rent.html

> *"A beautiful place—enjoyed our stay immensely. Great place for storytelling. Hope there wasn't a hidden tape recorder or that the walls don't talk."*
>
> From a Lookout's Guestbook

21 Pickett Butte Lookout

YOUR BEARINGS

10 miles northeast of Tiller
40 miles east of Canyonville
60 miles southeast of Roseburg
130 miles southeast of Eugene

AVAILABILITY November through May.

CAPACITY Maximum of four people—we suggest no more than two adults. The catwalk is narrow and the railing is low. Not suitable for small children. Dogs are allowed at the Lookout provided the owner picks up after them. It is important to supervise pets to assure protection of wildlife and plants in the vicinity.

DESCRIPTION Pickett Butte is a flat-topped structure that sits on a 40-foot tower. The railing around the structure is three feet high. Extreme caution should be taken at all times when on the catwalk. There is a pulley system on the tower to transport items from the ground to the cabin.

COST $40 per night.

RESERVATIONS Up to three consecutive

Pickett Butte Lookout

nights, noon to noon. The National Recreation Reservation Service (1-877-444-6777 or online at www.ReserveUSA.com).

To initiate you to the lookout experience, visit the historic Red Mountain Lookout, relocated to the grounds of the Tiller Ranger Station in 1985. Now fully restored, it serves as an interpretive site you may enjoy when stopping by for maps or other information prior to your stay. This cupola-style lookout was originally built on Red Mountain in the upper Cow Creek Valley in 1928. It is not for rent.

HOW TO GET THERE Travel time is approximately one hour from Canyonville, Oregon. Canyonville is located at exit 98 on Interstate 5. From Canyonville, travel east 24 miles to Tiller, Oregon via Highway 227. From Tiller, travel northeast on County Road 46 along the South Fork Umpqua River, and proceed three miles to Forest Road 3113, also called the Pickett Butte Road. Turn right, crossing the bridge. This turn is signed pickett butte lookout 7.

Stay on Road 3113, the main gravel road, which climbs steadily upward. After 5.2 miles turn left onto Forest Road 300. At the intersection, signed PICKETT BUTTE LOOKOUT 2, veer left, staying on Road 300.

This narrow road takes a dip and then resumes its uphill grade. One mile up Road 300, you will come to a gate at the lookout's entrance. Past the gate, the road becomes steeper and narrower. It takes you directly to the site, 0.25 mile from the gate.

In winter, check with the Ranger Station prior to making the trip to find out whether the road is open. The Forest Service sometimes plows the access road for guests but be prepared for snowpack.

ELEVATION 3200 feet

WHAT IS PROVIDED The cabin is well-equipped with a propane cook stove and fuel, propane heater, lights, and fridge. It also has a table, chairs, stool, and single bed. The outhouse is at the end of the driveway.

WHAT TO BRING Backpack or bag to use with pulley system, sleeping bags and pillows, drinking water, candles or lantern, matches, first aid kit, flashlight, garbage bag to pack out your trash, axe, shovel, pot and pans for cooking, dishes, utensils, food (the nearest store is 30 minutes away), toilet paper. Potable water is available at a spigot in front of the Tiller Ranger Station Office.

THE SETTING It is thrilling to be 41 feet up on a wooden tower, some 57 steps from ground to front door. Negotiating the steep stairway is easier going up than down. The views are subtle, yet captivating.

HISTORY Before the advent of airplane surveillance for fire detection, more than a dozen lookouts guarded the forests of the Tiller Ranger District. Today Pickett Butte and Acker Rock Lookout, which is also available for rent, are the only two that remain.

AROUND YOU Pickett Butte Lookout offers views of the entire Jackson Creek Drainage. Overlooking the diverse landscape of the Tiller Ranger District, there are expansive views of the Rogue-Umpqua Divide, which is south and east of Pickett Butte, and has scenic peaks and landmarks capped with snow until early summer.

FOR MORE INFORMATION
Umpqua National Forest
Tiller Ranger Station
27812 Tiller Trail Hwy
Tiller, OR 97484
(541) 825-3100
http://www.fs.fed.us/r6/umpqua/rec/bldg_rnt/rr2pickt.html

"A place where human structures compliment nature's structures."

Whisky Camp Guest, September, 1995

22 Whisky Camp

YOUR BEARINGS
20 miles east of Tiller
50 miles east of Canyonville
70 miles southeast of Roseburg
140 miles southeast of Eugene

AVAILABILITY Year-round.

CAPACITY Eight people maximum. Ideal for families.

DESCRIPTION A lovely two-room cabin with covered front porch.

COST $40 per night.

RESERVATIONS Up to seven consecutive nights, from noon to noon. The National Recreation Reservation Service (1-877-444-6777 or online at www.ReserveUSA.com).

HOW TO GET THERE Travel time is approximately one hour from Canyonville, Oregon. Canyonville is located at exit 98 on Interstate 5. From Canyonville, travel east 24 miles to Tiller, Oregon via Highway 227. From the Tiller Ranger Station travel northeast on County Road 46 along the South Fork Umpqua River for 5 miles to Jackson Creek Road 29. Turn right (southeast) over the bridge onto Road 29, which is a paved, two-lane road paralleling Jackson Creek. Follow Road 29 for 9.7 miles to Road 2925. (At this point you may wish to take a short side trip to the world's tallest sugar pine tree—the route is clearly signed). Follow Road 2925 for 6.5 miles to the five-way junction. Take Road 3114-600 for 1.5 miles to Road 3114-645. This road has a locked gate and is the entrance to Whisky Camp. The red cabin is a short skip down the driveway.

ELEVATION 3500 feet

WHAT IS PROVIDED The two-room cabin is furnished with one double bed and two single beds. Amenities include a heater, lanterns, cooking stove with oven, and a refrigerator—all powered with propane, which is provided.

WHAT TO BRING Sleeping bags and pillows, extra blankets, drinking water, candles or lantern, matches, first aid kit, flashlight, insect repellent, garbage bag to pack out your trash, axe, shovel, pot and pans for cooking, dishes, utensils, food (the nearest store is 30 minutes away), toilet paper. Potable water is available at a spigot in front of the Tiller Ranger Station Office.

THE SETTING Quiet. It is a wonderful place to bring a family. The highlight of the cabin is its large, sheltered front porch. A perfect place for conversation or contemplation. The cabin, itself, nestles in a grove of incense cedar, facing southwest, and receives warm, dappled light throughout the day. A peeled-rail fence encircles the grounds. To the west of the cabin you will find a vault toilet and a shelter built by the Civilian Conservation Corps in the 1930s.

Whiskey Camp

HISTORY Experience what the life of a Forest Service fire guard was like before the days of roads and aerial fire detection. This cabin was the summer home of fire guards whose primary duties were to spot smoke, fight fires, give respite to the lookout guard, maintain phone lines and trails, and patrol the forest.

AROUND YOU A forest of incense cedar, pine, and fir surrounds Whisky Camp. Visitors are within a short driving distance of historic Butler Butte and the Scenic Road along the Rogue-Umpqua Divide.

FOR MORE INFORMATION
Umpqua National Forest
Tiller Ranger District
27812 Tiller-Trail Hwy.
Tiller, Oregon 97484
(541) 825-3100
http://www.fs.fed.us/r6/umpqua/rec/bldg_rnt/rr2whisk.html

"Give me the splendid silent sun with all his beams full-dazzling."

Walt Whitman, "Miracles"

23 Butler Butte Cabin

YOUR BEARINGS Two hours from Canyonville, Oregon. Canyonville is located south of Eugene, Oregon at exit 98 on Interstate 5.

AVAILABILITY Year-round.

CAPACITY Up to eight people, maximum.

DESCRIPTION A one-room cabin.

COST $40 per night.

RESERVATION Up to seven consecutive nights, from noon to noon. The National Recreation Reservation Service (1-877-444-6777 or online at www.ReserveUSA.com).

SAFETY CONDITIONS Forest Service roads are generally one-lane gravel roads with pullouts. Many people frequent these roads, driving logging trucks, forestry vehicles, and recreational campers. Drive slowly and stay to the right side of the road at all times. Be alert and drive defensively. Be prepared for snow-packed roads during the winter months.

HOW TO GET THERE From the Tiller Ranger District office, take County Road 46, South Umpqua Road, for five miles to Jackson Creek Road 29. Follow Road 29 for 9.7 miles to the junction with Road 2925.

Follow Road 2925 for 6.5 miles to the five-way junction of Roads 2925, 600, 700, and 800. From here, there are two routes to choose from. One route is to follow Road 800 for 2.5 miles to the junction with the 810 Road and then to follow the 810 Road to the cabin. Although this is the shortest and most direct route, road 800 is an old logging road with water bars cut into it. Therefore, it may not be the best choice for passenger cars. For the other route, follow the 700 Road for approximately 6 miles to the junction with the 800 Road at Tucker Gap. The 700 and 800 Roads form a big loop and this is where they rejoin one another. At this point you will be making a sharp switchback turn to your right, onto the 800 Road. Follow the 800 Road for 2 miles to the junction with the 810 Road and then follow the 810 Road to the cabin. These roads are not plowed in the winter. During an average winter, generally up to a five-mile snowmobile, cross-country ski, or snowshoe excursion is required to reach the cabin.

ELEVATION 5500 feet

WHAT IS PROVIDED The one-room cabin is furnished with a double bed and two single beds. Amenities include a heater, lights, a cook stove with oven, and a refrigerator, all powered by propane—which is provided. There is a vault toilet at the site. You will find an outdoor fire pit and barbeque. A picnic table is provided.

WHAT TO BRING Sleeping bags and pillows, extra blankets, drinking water, candles or lantern, matches, first aid kit, flashlight, insect repellent, garbage bag to pack out your trash, axe, shovel, pot and pans for cooking, dishes, utensils, food (the nearest store is 30 minutes away), toilet paper. Potable water is available at a spigot in front of the Tiller Ranger Station Office.

Butler Butte Cabin

HISTORY The Butler Butte cabin was built in 1942 as an Aircraft Warning System (AWS) station. The site was chosen as a strategic location to watch for Japanese planes and balloons loaded with incendiary devices, meant to set our American west coast forests on fire. Lookout guards were stationed on mountaintops to watch for any signs of aerial invasion or fire. A 20-foot Lookout tower was built on the site in 1932. Eleven years later, after the threat of attack subsided, the lookout and cabin were used for forest fire observation purposes. Sadly, the lookout was burned prior to 1958 because it was no longer needed for fire detection—and unfortunately, the recreation rental program had not yet come into being. The cabin for rent is where the lookout guard lived and is the original structure from 1942. The lookout tower itself, adjacent to the cabin, was a separate structure and is no longer in existence.

AROUND YOU Activities in the area include hiking and horseback riding in the summer months and snowmobiling and cross-country skiing in the winter. The cabin is within a short driving distance of the scenic road along the Rogue-Umpqua Divide.

FOR MORE INFORMATION
Umpqua National Forest
Tiller Ranger District
27812 Tiller-Trail Hwy.
Tiller, OR 97484
(541) 825-3100
http://www.fs.fed.us/r6/umpqua/rec/bldg_rnt/rr2butle.html

———————————————— ❧ ————————————————

"The sky is the daily bread of the eyes."
Ralph Waldo Emerson, *Journal*, May 25, 1843

24 Fairview Peak Lookout Tower

YOUR BEARINGS
40 miles southeast of Cottage Grove
100 miles northeast of Roseburg
200 miles southeast of Portland
65 miles southeast of Eugene

AVAILABILITY Fairview Peak Lookout Tower is located in snow country. Due to limited access, this facility is only available from around mid-June/early-July through the end of October/beginning November, depending on snow accumulations. The stay limit at Fairview Peak Lookout Tower is three nights. Fairview Peak Lookout may be unavailable during peak fire season, typically August 1 through September 30. Should Fire Management decide to utilize the fire tower as a staffed lookout, your reservation will be rescheduled, and if necessary a refund will be made.

CAPACITY Up to four people, maximum.

DESCRIPTION A 14 x 14-foot cabin atop a 53-foot tower. The Lookout affords 360-degree views.

COST $40 per night. Fees collected for recreation rental facilities are for maintenance of the site. Collected fees may go to the replacement of furnishings, repair of the structure, and the addition of amenities.

RESERVATION Up to three consecutive nights, from 2:00 P.M. to noon. Call the toll-free National Recreation Reservation Service at 1-877-444-6777 or make reservations online at www.ReserveUSA.com.

SAFETY CONDITIONS Forest Service roads are generally one-lane gravel roads with pullouts. Many people frequent these roads, driving logging trucks, forestry vehicles, and recreational campers. Drive slowly and stay to the right side of the road at all times. Be alert and drive defensively. Be prepared for snow-packed roads during the winter months.

HOW TO GET THERE Take Row River Road 2400 east 19 miles to Brice Creek Road 2470. Keep right and continue on Brice Creek Road for 12 miles to Noonday Road 2212. Turn right on Road 2212 and travel for 8.8 miles to Champion Saddle. At Champion Saddle, stay left, traveling on Sharps Creek Road 2460 for 1.1 miles to Fairview Lookout Road 2460-773. Turn right on this road and follow for 1.2 miles to the end. The last 0.25 mile is rough and steep, and is recommended for high-clear-

Fairview Peak Lookout Tower

ance vehicles only. Use low gear and drive slowly and deliberately. Fairview Peak is located within the Slide Patented Mining Claim and is private property. However, the side of the mountain summit where the lookout tower is located is Forest Service property.

ELEVATION 5933 feet

WHAT IS PROVIDED One single bunk bed (lower bed is a double futon) to sleep a total of 3. There is room on the floor to sleep one more but you need to bring your own sleeping bag and pad. Propane-powered refrigerator, cook stove, heating stove, and lights. The Forest Service provides the propane fuel. A vault toilet is located at the base of the tower. There is a pulley system to help you raise your belongings up the steps. Also provided are a fire extinguisher, smoke detector, broom and dustpan.

WHAT TO BRING Water for all your drinking, cooking, and washing needs for the length of your stay. Sleeping bags and pillows, extra blankets, drinking water, candles or lantern, matches, first aid kit, flashlight, insect repellent, garbage bag to pack out your trash, axe, shovel, pot and pans for cooking, dishes, utensils, food (the nearest store is 30 minutes away), toilet paper.

HISTORY The Fairview Peak site was historically occupied as a fire lookout since the 1920's. Between 1958 and 1968 Fairview Peak was used as an Air Force radar facility. Today, Fairview Peak is host to private radio towers and Fairview Peak Lookout Tower. While aerial surveillance has replaced the need for continual summer lookout staffing, the lookout tower is often staffed during high fire danger, frequently during the months of August and September.

Musick Mine and Bohemia City, now private land, were one of the most productive mines in the Bohemia Mining District. The area is surrounded by rugged summits up to 6,000 feet in elevation and steep timbered slopes. Bohemia City can be viewed from Fairview Peak Lookout and from Bohemia Mountain trail.

AROUND YOU The 53-foot tall tower sports a 360-degree view with a vista unlike any west of the Cascade Range. On a clear day, one can see north to Mount Hood, south to Crater Lake and Mt. McLaughlin, and east to many prominent peaks in the Cascade Range.

Bohemia Mountain Trail leads up a steep grade to the rocky summit of Bohemia Mountain, the highest point on the Cottage Grove Ranger District. It is a 0.75-mile trail with grades averaging 15–20 percent. One-way trip duration is 45 minutes to one hour and no water is available. Because the mountain is just across from the Lookout, a similar view can bee seen of the Cascade Range from this location.

FOR MORE INFORMATION
Cottage Grove Ranger Station
78405 Cedar Park Rd
Cottage Grove, Oregon 97424
(541) 767-5000
http://www.fs.fed.us/r6/umpqua/rec/bldg_rnt/fairview1.htm

"It is absolutely beautiful up here on the ridge. I was born and raised in Oregon and I never knew that this peaceful and serene place existed..."

From the Cabin's Guestbook

25 Musick Guard Station

YOUR BEARINGS Nestled in Oregon's Central Cascades, Musick Guard Station sits atop a narrow forested ridge that rises between Fairview Peak and Grouse Mountain, 50 miles southeast of Cottage Grove.

AVAILABILITY Musick Guard Station is located in snow country. Due to limited access, this facility is only available from around mid-June/early-July through the end of October/beginning November, depending on snow accumulations. The stay limit at Musick Guard Station is seven nights.

CAPACITY Up to 10 people, maximum.

DESCRIPTION The expansive views of the area including that of Champion Creek, which was not visible from any other lookout or covered by any other guard station, made this location ideal.

COST $40 per night. Fees collected for recreation rental facilities are for maintenance of the site.

Musick Guard Station

Collected fees may go to the replacement of furnishings, repair of the structure, and the addition of amenities.

RESERVATION Up to seven consecutive nights, from 2:00 P.M. to noon. The National Recreation Reservation Service (1-877-444-6777 or online at www.ReserveUSA.com.

SAFETY CONDITIONS Forest Service roads are generally one-lane gravel roads with pullouts. Many people frequent these roads, driving logging trucks, forestry vehicles, and recreational campers. Drive slowly and stay to the right side of the road at all times. Be alert and drive defensively. Be prepared for snow-packed roads during the winter months.

HOW TO GET THERE Take Row River Road 2400, east 19 miles to Brice Creek Road 2470. Keep right and continue on Brice Creek Road for 12 miles to Noonday Road 2212. Turn right on Road 2212 and travel for 8.8 miles to Champion Saddle. Stay to your left, traveling on Sharps Creek Road 2460, for 0.4-mile to Road 2460-480 on your right. There is a gate at this junction and Musick Guard Station is 100 yards up this road. Parking is limited and we discourage parking in the road.

ELEVATION 5000 feet

WHAT IS PROVIDED Inside the cabin you'll find wooden bunks, without mattresses, to sleep up to ten people. Also provided are a wood heat stove and wood cook stove, four chairs, a table, broom, dustpan, fire extinguisher, and smoke detector. There is a new vault toilet outside. The fireplace is a replica of the historic Civilian Conservation Corps design. You will also find an outdoor picnic table. Please note: there is neither water nor lights available.

WHAT TO BRING Sleeping bags and pillows, extra blankets, drinking water, candles or lantern, matches, first aid kit, flashlight, insect repellent, garbage bag to pack out your trash, axe, shovel, pot and pans for cooking, dishes, utensils, food (the nearest store is 30 minutes away), toilet paper.

HISTORY The Civilian Conservation Corps constructed Musick Guard Station in 1934 to provide fire protection to the Bohemia Mining area. Musick Mine and Bohemia City, now private land, were one of the most productive mines in the Bohemia Mining District.

Musick Guard Station became an important public contact point and administrative center for the Forest Service and was used by Bohemia Ranger District (now known as Cottage Grove Ranger District) fireguard, packer, and District Ranger between the years 1933 and 1934. Later it was used as summer barracks for trail crews and firefighting crews. The Guard Station was named after the nearby Musick Mine, a major producing mine in the late 1800s and early 1900s.

AROUND YOU There is an abundance of recreational opportunities surrounding Musick Guard Station. Nearby Fairview Peak is approximately 5933 feet in elevation and provides 360-degree views from the top. The tower is staffed during peak fire season and is rented between mid-June and late October when not being used by fire staff.

Musick Mine and Bohemia City, now private land, were one of the most productive mines in the Bohemia Mining District. The area is surrounded by rugged summits up to 6000 feet in elevation and steep timbered slopes. Bohemia City can be viewed from Fairview Peak Lookout and from Bohemia Mountain trail.

Bohemia Mountain Trail leads up a steep grade to the rocky summit of Bohemia Mountain, the highest point on the Cottage Grove Ranger District. It is a 0.75-mile trail with grades averaging 15–20 percent. One-way trip duration is 45 minutes to one hour and no water is available. Because the mountain is just across from the lookout, a similar view can bee seen of the Cascade Range from that location.

FOR MORE INFORMATION
Cottage Grove Ranger Station
78405 Cedar Park Rd
Cottage Grove, Oregon 97424
(541) 767-5000
http://www.fs.fed.us/r6/umpqua/rec/bldg_rnt/musick1.htm

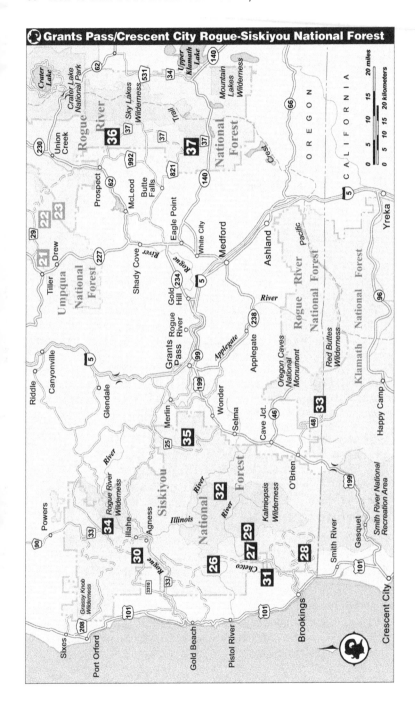

Rogue-Siskiyou National Forest

*"I am he that walks with the tender and growing night,
I call to the earth and the sea half-held by the night."*

Walt Whitman, "Song of Myself"

26 Snow Camp Lookout

It was heartbreaking news to hear that the beloved Snow Camp Lookout was destroyed in the Biscuit Fire during the summer of 2002. Yet, it's heartwarming news indeed to learn this popular rental facility is in the process of being rebuilt—an effort made possible by the countless hours volunteered by Don Hartley, owner of Don Hartley Construction in Crescent City, California. Don provided invaluable technical expertise in all phases of the reconstruction, from design and planning through on-site supervision and actual construction. Don had been a frequent visitor to the former lookout and he has been committed to assuring that this opportunity would not be lost forever. Thank you, Don!

YOUR BEARINGS

25 miles southeast of Gold Beach
30 miles northeast of Brookings
60 miles north of Crescent City
180 miles west of Medford

AVAILABILITY May to October.

CAPACITY A maximum of five people, though two would be more comfortable. Good for families.

DESCRIPTION 15 x 15-foot room with surrounding deck and railing, and 360-degree views.

COST $40 per night plus reservation fee.

RESERVATIONS Call the toll-free National Recreation Reservation Service at 1-877-444-6777, or make reservations online at www.ReserveUSA.com.

HOW TO GET THERE There are two well-signed, though distinctly different, routes to the lookout, both via the town of Brookings. One follows an inland route and the other follows the coastal highway, US 101. Each takes 1.5 to 2 hours driving time from the Chetco Ranger District office.

The advantage of the inland route is that you travel through the beautiful Chetco River Valley, though there are more miles of gravel roads than via Highway 101.

The advantage of the 101 route is that it travels 26 miles along the scenic coastal highway, offering spectacular views of the Pacific Ocean and its unique sea stacks just off-shore. There are several Oregon state parks along this drive with spectacular vista points.

Inland Route: From the Chetco Ranger District office, in downtown Brookings, Oregon, travel south on US Highway 101 for one mile to the North Bank Road (not shown on map). Watch for the sign NORTH BANK ROAD just before the bridge over the Chetco River. Turn left here. The North Bank Road makes an immediate right turn and heads upriver. The road is paved, winding and well-traveled.

After nine miles from Highway 101, you will reach the border of the Siskiyou National Forest. Here the road becomes Forest Road 1376. This is a single-lane, paved road, with turnouts and narrow bridges. It offers beautiful vistas of the Chetco River. The river is easily accessible via the picnic areas and campgrounds you pass along the way.

After 16 miles from Highway 101, Road 1376 crosses the South Fork Chetco River bridge. Continue on 1376 to Mile Post 18 where, at a fork, you will veer left toward Snow Camp—it is signed. After 3.1

Snow Camp Lookout

miles from Mile Post 18, turn right, still on Road 1376. Proceed for another 5.5 miles to the lookout entrance—on your left at the yellow gate. Unlock the gate and go 0.5 mile to the lookout parking lot. A wheelbarrow is available to help haul your gear the 200 yards up a steep, rocky grade to the cabin.

US 101 Route: From the Chetco Ranger District office, travel 26 miles north on US 101 to the Hunter Creek Road. Turn right (east). Go five miles on the paved, two-lane county road, to where it becomes Forest Road 3680, and its surface becomes gravel. Go 18.5 miles on Road 3680 to its junction with Forest Road 1376. Turn right (uphill) onto Road 1376 for 1.2 miles to the yellow gate. Unlock the gate and proceed 0.5 mile to the lookout parking lot.

Along the route you may notice that the rocks in the roadcuts are shiny greenish-blue, and erode to reddish-orange soils. This is serpentine rock which was once on the ocean floor. Millions of years ago this rock was pushed upward, and it now caps many of the high mountain ridges in this region. It supports a unique community of rare trees and plants.

ELEVATION 4223 feet

WHAT IS PROVIDED A double bed with a mattress, a table and chairs, counters and cupboards, a woodstove, and split wood stacked outside the door. In the center of the lookout is an Osborne Fire Finder. On the walls above the windows are beautiful, routed, wooden signs of key geographic place-names in the region. A picnic table and a chemical toilet are just outside.

WHAT TO BRING No water is available so bring all you will need.

THE SETTING Overlooks the Pistol River Drainage, the 180,000-acre Kalmiopsis Wilderness, the Big Craggies Botanical Area, and, incidentally, the Pacific Ocean—which of course glistens in the moonlight. With light pouring in from all sides, you'll soon understand how an eagle feels in its nest.

Adjacent to the lookout is a communications building and tower. Though a bit of an eyesore, they do not significantly obstruct the view.

HISTORY Snow Camp Lookout was built in 1958, and was used as a lookout until 1972. It was then reincarnated in 1990 as a recreational rental property. The first lookout on this site was built in 1924 and was used during World War II to detect enemy aircraft.

In the morning of September 9, 1942, Nobuo Fujita became the only man to make an enemy bombing run over the continental United States. Fujita placed his will and a lock of his hair in a box to be sent back to Japan. He then put his four-hundred-year-old samurai sword aboard a single-engine float plane, and took off from submarine I-25 off the coast of Cape Blanco, Oregon, convinced he was facing certain death. He flew 50 miles southeast over a wooded area where he dropped one incendiary bomb on the slopes of Wheeler Ridge. He saw flames spreading through the trees, flew on, then dropped another bomb before flying back to his submarine.

His attack was intended to start a massive forest fire that would strike panic into the heart of America, and serve as a counter-strike to the US bombing raid on Tokyo the previous April. However, a fire-lookout guard spotted the smoke and alerted a fire crew, and the fire was soon brought under control.

Three weeks later, Fujita launched another attack, this time on Grassy Knob outside the coastal community of Port Orford, but due to wet conditions that year, it too fizzled. Twenty years later he returned to Brookings as an honored guest, bringing with him the same 400-year-old samurai sword, a traditional Japanese symbol of peace and friendship. The sword is on display at the Chetco Community Library, 420 Alder Street, Brookings, Oregon.

AROUND YOU Snow Camp Trail (1103) is accessible from the parking lot. It offers an intimate look at the unique geology and plant communities of this area.

Fairview Meadow, just northwest of the lookout on Trail 1103, is thought to be the result of burning by Native Americans and early settlers despite the fact that this area gets up to 100 inches of rainfall annually. But it is a lovely result.

In Fairview Meadow is the Enchanted Forest, a hauntingly beautiful stand of old-growth Douglas fir. The lichens hanging from the trees take all their nutrients and water from the air.

To hike to Snow Camp Meadow, take Trail 1103 from the parking area. If you keep your eyes peeled, you may see elk, deer, bear, and blue grouse. Look for western tree frogs and caddis flies in the pond at Snow Camp Meadow.

About 0.5 mile east of the lookout you will find a bog which is home to the cobra plant, *Darlingtonia californica*. It survives by trapping insects inside its tubular leaves and digesting them with the aid of bacteria, to provide itself with nutrients such as nitrogen, which is not available in the serpentine soils.

The lookout itself has been through several reincarnations and may have more to go. Take good care of it.

FOR MORE INFORMATION
Gold Beach Ranger District
29279 Ellensburg Avenue
Gold Beach, OR 97444
(541) 247-3600
http://www.fs.fed.us/r6/rogue-siskiyou/
recreation/cabins/snow-camp.shtml

"...beautiful setting and the warmth of fellow travelers gone before."

From the Cabin's Guestbook, December 1994

27 Packers Cabin

YOUR BEARINGS

25 miles northeast of Brookings
35 miles southeast of Gold Beach
50 miles north of Crescent City
225 miles southwest of Eugene

AVAILABILITY Year-round, weather permitting.

CAPACITY Up to ten people, though that would be taking the cabin's name a bit too literally—four to six would be much more comfortable. Ideal for families.

DESCRIPTION Historic and charming Packer's Cabin is "barrier-free." The 28 x 16-foot, 3-room facility has ramps, wooden porch and railing, decks, wide doorways, and door handles to make the structure as accessible as possible.

COST $20 per night. This money is used for maintenance and renovation of the cabin.

RESERVATIONS The cabin is reserved from noon to noon on a first come, first-come, first-served basis. Call toll-free the National Recreation Reservation Service (1-877-444-6777), or make reservations online at www.ReserveUSA.com.

HOW TO GET THERE Travel time is about 1.5 hours from Brookings, Oregon. From the Chetco Ranger District office, in downtown Brookings, Oregon, travel south on US Highway 101 for one mile to the North Bank Road (not shown on map). Watch for the sign NORTH BANK ROAD just before the bridge over the Chetco River. Turn left here. The North Bank Road makes an immediate right turn and heads upriver. The road is paved, winding, and well-traveled.

After nine miles from Highway 101, you will reach the border of the Siskiyou National Forest. Here the road becomes Forest Road 1376. This is a single-lane, paved road, with turnouts and narrow bridges. It offers beautiful vistas of the Chetco River. The river is easily accessible via the picnic areas and campgrounds you pass along the way.

After 16 miles from Highway 101, Forest Road 1376 crosses the South Fork Chetco River Bridge. Continue one mile west to Forest Road 1917. Turn right onto Road 1917 and travel six more miles northeast on this narrow, moderately steep, gravel road. A sign indicates this road is not accessible to trailers, though it is suitable for passenger cars.

Stay right on Forest Road 1917 at its junction with Road 060. The driveway to the cabin is 2.5 miles ahead on the right side of the road. The only other destination on Forest Road 1917 is the Quail Prairie Lookout, 3.5 miles (according to the sign) east of Packers Cabin.

ELEVATION 2073 feet

WHAT IS PROVIDED Woodstove and firewood, folding chairs, benches, shelves, and a large wooden table. The guestbook is a treasure. There are two small bedrooms. One is furnished with three sets of bunk beds stacked three high, sleeping a total of nine. The other bedroom has a double bunk and a single bunk.

Outside you will find a vault toilet, picnic tables, and a fire ring. The cabin and outhouse have ramps, wide doorways, and special door handles which make it fully accessible for wheelchair users.

WHAT TO BRING Bring camping equipment and sleeping bags. There is neither electricity nor drinking water at the site, so bring a lantern, flashlights, and plenty of potable water.

THE SETTING This historic outpost is sequestered on the edge of a forest; perfect for artists needing a place to just be. On one side of the yard is a thick cluster of tall Douglas-fir trees, on the other, mature tanoak. To the north there is a natural spring set in a small meadow surrounded by low brush.

HISTORY The cabin was built about 1930 as field headquarters for the backcountry packers who, on horseback or by mule train, regularly supplied the lookout guards and field crews with food and equipment. The structure was renovated in 1990 with funds from a Regional Forester Challenge Grant and the help of volunteers from Brookings and Harbor.

As you sit in the front yard on Long Ridge at Packers Cabin, listening to the water gurgle at the natural spring and the acorns fall, you are playing your part in maintaining the long history of this well-loved cabin in the Siskiyou Mountains.

AROUND YOU Quail Prairie Lookout, at an elevation of 3033 feet, is, according to the wooden sign, 3.5 miles east of Packers Cabin, on Forest Road 1917. This lookout is staffed from July to October. You are welcome to visit the site and enjoy the view from its 50-foot tower: the Chetco River Valley, Big Craggies and part of Kalmiopsis Wilderness.

In the natural openings of the forest watch for Roosevelt elk, blacktail deer, black bear, wild turkey, quail, blue grouse, and red-tailed hawks. The best times are, of course, the early morning hours and at twilight.

For mountain bikers, the Long Ridge Loop (8.6 miles), along Forest Roads 060 and 1917, offers a scenic trip on graveled surfaces.

FOR MORE INFORMATION
Chetco Ranger District
P.O. Box 4580
539 Chetco Ave.
Brookings, OR 97415
(541) 412-6000
http://www.fs.fed.us/r6/roguesiskiyou/recreation/cabins/packers.shtml

---

"We want to rest, we need to rest and allow the earth to rest. We need to reflect and to discover the mystery that lives in us..."

U.N. Environmental Sabbath Program

28 Ludlum House

YOUR BEARINGS
16 miles southeast of Brookings
50 miles southeast of Gold Beach
50 miles north of Crescent City
170 miles west of Medford

AVAILABILITY Year-round, weather permitting.

CAPACITY The house can comfortably hold eight people, and less comfortably, up to 30. Ideal for families.

DESCRIPTION The newly constructed two-story Ludlum House is scenically located at the confluence of Wheeler Creek and the Winchuck River. The site is both shaded and open with a grassy lawn. It has two rooms (with 3/4 dividing wall upstairs); a ground floor surrounding covered porch; a huge wood stove, and minimal interior furnishings (no beds). The first floor and grounds are wheelchair accessible. Maximum use capacity is 30 indoors, and 60 total for the house and surrounding grounds. There is a dry sink and food preparation counter. There is no electricity, but basic lighting is provided with several propane and battery powered lanterns.

COST $40 per night for groups up to 10 persons. There is an additional charge of $3 per person for groups over 10. This money is used for maintenance, furnishings, and renovation of the house. Maximum stay is six consecutive nights.

RESERVATIONS Call toll-free the National Recreation Reservation Service (1-877-444-6777) or make your reservations online at www.ReserveUSA.com. The house is reserved from noon to noon on a first-come, first-served basis.

HOW TO GET THERE The route to Ludlum House is a two-lane paved road most of the way. Go south from Brookings on US 101 for eight miles to the Winchuck River Road (County Road 896). Turn left (east), and after six miles Road 896 becomes Forest Road 1107. Go 2.3 miles to the junction of Road 1108. Veer left and uphill, onto Forest Road 1108. It too is paved at first, though it narrows and turns to gravel along Wheeler Creek. The driveway of Ludlum House, which is on the right side of the road, is 2.5 miles from the 1108 junction. The house is 200 yards down the driveway.

ELEVATION 360 feet

WHAT IS PROVIDED Drinking water from a hand pump, picnic tables, fire rings, a vault toilet, and group use area are outside. Firewood is provided for the woodstove.

WHAT TO BRING Bring camping equipment, flashlights, cooking/eating utensils, sleeping bags, and pads for comfort. Bring size D batteries for the lanterns.

HISTORY Built in the 1930s—by most accounts in 1937 or 1938—the cabin was originally a homestead. The last private owner of the house and property, and the person from whom it derives its name, was Robert C. Ludlum. He was an oil company executive who, in 1951, quit his job in Japan, returned to the United States, and, with his wife and two children, moved into the house.

The family moved to California the next year, though Ludlum returned to the Winchuck from time to time to work on his place and spend time here. He eventually sold it to the Forest Service in 1969.

Over the years, Ludlum House has developed a loyal group of visitors and guests who return to the cabin again and again. It has been the site of weddings, baptisms, reunions, and many other of life's significant events. In recent years it has twice served as a base for crews battling major forest fires in the area: the July Fire in 1986 and the Chrome Fire in 1990.

AROUND YOU Amid groves of myrtle and redwood, this homestead is in the Coast Range of the Siskiyou Mountains in southwestern Oregon. The Pacific Ocean is just a 30-minute drive away.

A mature Oregon myrtle grove shades the cabin's large parking area—which is suitable for passenger cars and recreational vehicles. Several picnic tables surround the campfire pit. Other picnic tables are scattered amid the trees. The front porch is just 100 feet from Wheeler Creek.

The confluence of Wheeler Creek and the Winchuck River is a short walk from the driveway gate, down the spur road. A sunny, gravel beach makes a fine spot to enjoy the water and the scent of the myrtle trees. The Oregon myrtle, from which we get the culinary bay leaf, often grows in clumps of five to ten stems, all coming from one root.

The Winchuck River is renowned for its winter-run steelhead, though fishing is allowed downstream of Wheeler Creek only. Licenses are available in Brookings sports shops or from the Oregon Department of Fish and Wildlife.

Wheeler Creek is a protected spawning ground for fall chinook and winter steelhead, and a year-round home to cutthroat and rainbow trout. Typically, chinooks start spawning here in October, depending on when the autumn rains begin. Steelhead can be spawning here as late as January. If you do see fish spawning, it is important not to disturb them.

To ensure a healthy population, the Forest Service asks anglers to release any fish measuring less than eight inches. These small fish are smolts, and if released will come back to this creek as adults. In their efforts to improve fish habitat, the Forest Service has installed a variety of devices in the river to restore the natural mix of pools and riffles in the stream.

On the hill directly across the road from Ludlum House is a stand of old-growth redwoods. Though there is no trail, the steep hike is a rewarding one. Just across Wheeler Creek is an old apple orchard which still produces delicious apples in the fall. It is a good place for a picnic any time of year.

Ludlum House

The ocean beaches are just a 30-minute drive, as is Redwood State Park in Northern California. Nearby hiking trails include: Chimney Camp Trail 1279; Sourdough Trail 1114; Oregon Redwoods Trail 1106 (barrier-free—wheelchair accessible) and Oregon Redwoods Trail 1107 (Hiking).

FOR MORE INFORMATION
Chetco Ranger District
P.O. Box 4580
539 Chetco Ave
Brookings, OR 97415
(541) 412-6000
http://www.fs.fed.us/r6/rogue-siskiyou/recreation/cabins/ludlum.shtml

"Man is rich in proportion to the number of things which he can afford to let alone."

Henry David Thoreau, *Walden*

29 Quail Prairie Lookout

YOUR BEARINGS Located 26 road miles northeast of Brookings, Oregon, overlooking the Kalmiopsis Wilderness.

AVAILABILITY Depending upon the weather, the Lookout is available June 15th through October 15th.

CAPACITY Four people maximum. Children under age 12 are not allowed.

DESCRIPTION Quail Prairie Fire Lookout is a 52-foot tall wooden tower with a 15 x 15-foot cabin structure on top. This is a primitive type experience (don't forget you have some stairs to climb!).

COST $50 per night. This money is used for maintenance and renovation of the lookout.

RESERVATIONS A maximum of three consecutive nights, reserved from noon to noon. Reservations will be accepted on a first-come, first-served basis. Call the toll-free National Recreation Reservation Service (1-877-444-6777) or make your reservations online at www.ReserveUSA.com.

HOW TO GET THERE To get to Quail Prairie Lookout from Brookings, travel US Hwy 101; turn east on North Bank Chetco River Road (County Road 784). In approximately 8 miles, past Loeb Sate Park, it becomes Forest Service road 1376. The pavement ends just beyond Little Redwood Campground (14 miles). Turn left after crossing the South Fork Bridge (16 miles from Brookings). Turn right on Forest Service road 1917 approximately one mile after the bridge. Follow Quail Prairie signs, staying on road 1917. The lookout is three miles beyond Packer's Cabin. Total driving distance is 26 miles.

Forest Service roads are generally one-lane gravel roads with pull-outs. Many people use these roads, including logging trucks, forestry workers, and recreational vehicles. Drive slowly, stay to the right side of the road at all times, and use pullouts. Above all, be alert and drive defensively.

ELEVATION 3033 feet

WHAT IS PROVIDED The cabin is furnished with one single bed, a wood burning stove (split wood is provided, however it is advised to bring your own kindling), a table, two chairs, solar shower, propane refrigerator, and stove. Cabinets for supplies and counters for food preparation are convenient features. Outside you will find a picnic table, fire ring and pit toilet.

WHAT TO BRING Water for all your cooking, drinking and washing needs. None is available. Kindling, warm clothing, camping gear, and food.

AROUND YOU From the tower, atop its very long legs, you can see the Chetco River Valley, the Big Craggies, and part of the Kalmiopsis Wilderness Area. In the natural openings of the forest watch for Roosevelt elk, black-tail deer, black bear, wild turkey, quail, grouse, and red-tailed hawks.

Packer's Cabin, another Forest Service rental, is just 3.5 miles west of the Lookout on Forest Service Road 1917.

FOR MORE INFORMATION
Chetco Ranger District
P.O. Box 4580
539 Chetco Ave
Brookings, OR 97415
(541) 412-6000
http://www.fs.fed.us/r6/
rogue-siskiyou/recreation/
cabins/index.shtml

Quail Prairie Lookout

> *"Give me a spark of Nature's fire. That's all the learning I desire."*
>
> Robert Burns

30 Lake of the Woods Lookout

YOUR BEARINGS

21 miles northeast of Gold Beach, Oregon

AVAILABILITY Depending upon the weather, the lookout is available May 1st through October 30th. During periods of intense summer storms a Forest Service Fire Officer may need to use the lookout for short periods of time to spot fires. We ask for your cooperation if this occurs. If you spot a fire while at the lookout, report it to the Forest Service immediately.

CAPACITY The building accommodates one to four people.

DESCRIPTION The R6 (Flat Roofed) cabin, originally a ground house, was flown by helicopter to the present location and placed on an 8-foot tower with a catwalk. It was placed on its current site in 1974. Lake of the Woods Lookout was staffed during fire season from 1974 to 1996. Declining fire budgets have not allowed for staffing of the lookout since this time.

COST $40 per night. This money is used for maintenance and renovation of the Lookout.

RESERVATIONS Reservations run from noon to noon and may not extend longer than five days. Call the toll-free National Recreation Reservation Service (1-877-444-6777) or make your reservations online at www.ReserveUSA.com.

HOW TO GET THERE To access the Lookout from the town of Gold Beach, Oregon travel on US Highway 101 turning east onto the South Bank of the Rogue River, County Road 595. This road becomes

Lake of the Woods Lookout

Forest Service Road 33. Travel approximately 27 miles along the river to the town of Agness. Continue approximately 9 miles on Forest Service Road 33 to Forest Service Road 3336. Turn left and travel approximately 8.2 miles to Forest Service Road 141. Pass through the gate and continue approximately 0.75 mile to the Lookout. Travel time from Gold Beach is approximately 1.5 hours.

When traveling in the National Forest please use caution. Forest Service roads are generally one-lane gravel roads with pullouts. Many people use these roads, including logging trucks, forestry workers, and recreational vehicles. Drive slowly, stay to the right side of the road at all times, and use pullouts. Above all, be alert and drive defensively.

ELEVATION 3419 feet

WHAT IS PROVIDED A propane stove, propane refrigerator, propane lights, a table and two chairs, a double bed, a footstool, broom, and fire extinguisher. An outhouse is located nearby. Also located adjacent to the Lookout are a picnic table and a fire pit for outdoor barbecues. (During periods of extreme fire danger there will be restrictions for outdoor burning).

WHAT TO BRING Camping gear, including bedding and cooking supplies. There is no water available so bring as much as you'll need for drinking, cooking, and washing.

HISTORY This Lookout was originally located on Barklow Mountain on the Powers Ranger District of the Siskiyou National Forest and moved to this site in 1974.

AROUND YOU Lake of the Woods Lookout provides a panoramic view, with vistas to the Pacific Ocean, Kalmiopsis and Wild Rogue Wildernesses, and the Wild and Scenic Illinois and Rogue River canyons. In addition to stargazing and storm watching, there are several old logging roads nearby beckoning mountain bikers and hikers. In springtime, Lake of the Woods is surrounded by wildflowers. As summer progresses the lake fills in with tall reeds and grasses. It eventually dries up completely, yet is reborn the following spring.

FOR MORE INFORMATION
Chetco Ranger District
P.O. Box 4580
539 Chetco Ave
Brookings, OR 97415
(541) 412-6000
http://www.fs.fed.us/r6/rogue-siskiyou/recreation/cabins/index.shtml

*"I go to nature to be soothed and healed, and to have
my senses put in tune once more."*

John Burroughs

31 Rainbow Creek Tent

YOUR BEARINGS The Tent is located near the end of the Chetco Gorge Trail
where Rainbow Creek enters the Chetco River. The site is situated near
the Chetco River.

AVAILABILITY The Rainbow Creek Tent site is available June 15th through
October 15th. Dates may vary somewhat depending on rain and river
depth.

CAPACITY 10 people maximum.

DESCRIPTION Instant camping in this rustic canvas walk-in tent, approximately 194 square feet in size. It has one bedroom with a detached
bath. It offers excellent views as well as privacy. No set-up is necessary.
The tent is situated under trees overlooking a small meadow. It is near
a sandy beach and excellent swimming hole. No trash removal is provided; this is a "pack-it-in, pack-it-out" site and a more primitive rental
experience.

COST $10 per night

RESERVATIONS Reservations may be made up to five consecutive nights,
from noon to noon. Call the toll-free National Recreation Reservation
Service (1-877-444-6777) or make your reservations online at
www.ReserveUSA.com. Reservations will be accepted on a first-come,
first-served basis.

HOW TO GET THERE Access is via an easy to moderate hike of 1.5 miles on
the Chetco Gorge Trail 1112, which requires a ford of the Chetco River
near the trailhead. From Brookings, Oregon travel US Hwy 101, to the
North Bank Chetco River Road (County Road 784) and turn east. This
road becomes Forest Service road 1376 past Loeb State Park in approximately 8 miles. The pavement ends just beyond Little Redwood
Campground (14 miles). Make a left turn after crossing the South Fork
Bridge (16 miles from Brookings). Turn left on Spur Road 170 (next
road junction past the road to the Chetco River Inn) to the Chetco
Gorge trailhead at the old Low Water Bridge site. Forest Service roads
are generally one-lane gravel roads with pullouts. Many people use
these roads, including logging trucks, forestry workers, and recreational vehicles. Drive slowly, stay to the right side of the road at all times,
and use pullouts. Above all, be alert and drive defensively.

Travel time from Brookings is about one hour to the trailhead

ELEVATION 160 feet

WHAT IS PROVIDED Sleeping cots for four, pit toilet, fire ring.

WHAT TO BRING Camping gear, including bedding and cooking supplies. There is no water available so bring as much as you'll need for drinking, cooking, and washing.

AROUND YOU You'll enjoy a refreshing dip on a hot summer day in the nearby swimming hole.

FOR MORE INFORMATION
Chetco Ranger District
P.O. Box 4580
539 Chetco Avenue
Brookings, OR 97415
(541) 412-6000
http://www.fs.fed.us/r6/rogue-siskiyou/recreation/cabins/rainbow-ck.shtml

---

"I have never set foot on this mountain that I didn't get the most wonderful feelings I have ever felt. It is truly a unique place."

From the Lookout's Guestbook

32 Pearsoll Peak Lookout

YOUR BEARINGS
25 miles northwest of Cave Junction
55 miles west of Grants Pass
85 miles west of Medford
100 miles west of Ashland
125 miles southwest of Roseburg

AVAILABILITY June 15 to September.

CAPACITY A maximum of four people, though two would be more comfortable.

DESCRIPTION 14 x 14-foot room with large windows. Recently restored, with expansive views.

COST No fee is charged for use of this rental. Contact the Ranger station for available dates and to book your reservation.

RESERVATIONS There is a Port-Orford-cedar road closure beginning October 1, requiring visitors to hike in seven miles via a trail from Onion Camp after this date. Available for as many as seven consecutive nights on a first-come, first-served basis. For availability, maps, and further information contact the Illinois Valley Ranger District (see "For More Information," below). This property is not on the reservation system as no fee is collected.

HOW TO GET THERE There are two routes to the lookout—one by road, the other by trail. The route by road is open only from June to September, and then only to four-wheel-drive, high-clearance vehicles.

Beginning at the Illinois Valley Ranger District office in Cave Junction, Oregon, take Highway 199 north 8.6 miles to the Illinois River Road (County Road 5070) in Selma. Turn left (west) onto County Road 5070 and travel 10.9 miles from Selma to Forest Road 087, the McCaleb Ranch turnoff.

At the McCaleb Ranch turnoff, veer left and cross the low-water bridge over the Illinois River. Proceed straight across the private-property section of the road, paralleling the West Fork of Rancherie Creek on Forest Road 087. Travel 5.2 miles from the Illinois River crossing to Chetco Pass. This section is very slow and rugged.

At Chetco Pass, turn right and proceed 1.2 miles to Billingslea Junction, which is signed. At this junction, veer left. Travel 0.7 mile to a very small parking area on the right side of the road. From here the lookout is in view.

Travel time from the Illinois River to the parking area is approximately 1.5 hours. Do not attempt to drive the final 300 yards of road beyond the parking area. This section is very dangerous and there are no turn-around spots. Hike up the road until you come to the Kalmiopsis Wilderness Boundary. At this point the road becomes a trail. Summer temperatures often reach 100 degrees. The hike from the park-

Pearsoll Peak Lookout

ing area takes only 35 to 45 minutes, but can be arduous in hot weather or high winds.

The alternative route is to backpack seven miles to the lookout from Onion Camp. To get to Onion Camp, travel 17 miles west on the Onion Camp Road (Forest Road 4201) from Highway 199. The turnoff is four miles south of Selma and five miles north of Cave Junction. Park at the trailhead at Onion Camp and follow the Kalmiopsis Rim Trail (1124.2).

The trail passes over Eagle Mountain, where it becomes an old mining road. Proceed to Chetco Pass and from there hike the road to Billingslea Junction, 1.2 miles. Veer left at the junction and proceed to the lookout.

ELEVATION 5098 feet

WHAT IS PROVIDED The table, chairs, bed, and cabinets have all been in this lookout since the 1930s. It also has a fire extinguisher, foot stool, oil lamp, and a map of the area. There is no stove or fridge nor any heat source.

In one of the drawers you will find a guestbook and a transcript of an interview with Albert Curnow, who staffed Pearsoll Peak Lookout in the 1930s. Tish did the interview more than a decade ago while working as an archaeologist for Siskiyou National Forest.

Also, note the two poems tacked to an inside wallpost. The first is "Mid-August at Sourdough Mountain Lookout," by Gary Snyder (see page 30). The second is anonymous, and also a gem.

The outhouse is just below the cabin. It was airlifted to this remote mountaintop by helicopter, and placed to afford users the finest view.

WHAT TO BRING No water is available so bring plenty. A spring is located about a mile down the main road from the lookout—watch for it on the way up. If you want to drink this water, use a filter or boil it. Bring a camp stove and fuel. Pack for hot days, and sharp, crisp summer nights.

HISTORY Mining activity in the Chetco Pass area during the Great Depression led to the construction of the first road into Pearsoll Peak. During World War II, the flat below the main saddle was used by the US Army as an enemy-plane detection site. Some evidence of this camp remains.

Pearsoll Peak is one of eight remaining lookouts in Siskiyou National Forest, and one of only two in the Illinois Valley Ranger District. Known as an L-4, this lookout was built in 1954, replacing an earlier cupola-style cabin constructed here in 1933. Prior to that Pearsoll Peak was the site of a primitive fire-lookout tent camp. The L-4 lookout kit could be ordered for $500 from Spokane, Washington, or Portland, Oregon. The L-4 models were also called "Aladdins" after their principal manufacturer. The lookout kit was designed with simplicity in mind; parts were numbered and blue prints were provided. The kit came ready to load on the backs of pack mules, the standard mode of transport into this and other remote Pacific Northwest mountaintops.

In 1973 the lookout was shut down, and was used thereafter only during periods of high fire danger. By the late 1980s, exposure and lack of use nearly led to its demise. But the story has a happy ending. Recognizing its charm and historic significance, the people of the Illinois Valley Ranger District, assisted by local volunteers and members of the Sand Mountain Society, united their skills and desires. Together, in 1991, they completely restored the lookout.

Now, in its full glory, the lookout is listed on the National Register of Historic Places and the National Register of Historic Lookouts. The site was dedicated in 1994 and has been available as a rental since then.

AROUND YOU Pearsoll Peak Lookout sits in a rugged and somewhat inaccessible section of the forest, just 197 feet outside the Kalmiopsis Wilderness boundary. The lookout is perched on an exposed peak that has steep cliffs on all sides. The cabin overlooks the Kalmiopsis Wilderness Area, and offers exceptional views of Vulcan Peak, Chetco Peak, Eagle Mountain, Canyon Peak and, on a very clear day, Mount Shasta.

PORT-ORFORD-CEDAR ROOT DISEASE The highly prized Port-Orford-cedar is native to southwestern Oregon and northwestern California. The tree is widely used for landscape plantings, hedges and windbreaks throughout the Northwest. A root fungus began killing ornamentals as early as 1922, and by 1952 had spread throughout most of the cedar's native range. Despite this, the watersheds of Rancherie Creek and its tributaries, en route to Pearsoll Peak Lookout, still have significant stands of healthy trees.

The fungus is spread by water-borne spores, making the risk of contamination greatest during the rainy season. Once infected, the trees die. You can help limit the spread of this disease by taking simple precautions required by the Illinois Valley Ranger District. As a prerequisite to the issuance of your permit, before using the Pearsoll Peak Road, please wash your vehicle, especially the undercarriage and tires. There is a car wash at a service station in Cave Junction, or you may use the wash facility at the Illinois Valley Ranger Station, on the south edge of Cave Junction.

FOR MORE INFORMATION
Illinois Valley Ranger District
Pam Bode, District Ranger
26568 Redwood Hwy
Cave Junction, OR 97523
(541) 592-4000

"Autumn is a second spring when every leaf's a flower."
Albert Camus

33 Bolan Mountain Lookout

YOUR BEARINGS

30 miles southeast of Cave Junction, Oregon.

AVAILABILITY The lookout is available for rent during the snow-free season, which is typically mid-July to mid-October.

CAPACITY Up to four people can stay at the lookout at any one time, although one or two would be much more comfortable.

DESCRIPTION Bolan Mountain Lookout is a 14 x 14-foot 1953 L-4 style cabin at ground level atop Bolan Mountain. Parking is just below the lookout. It sits atop a high peak with sharp cliffs all around. For safety reasons, it is therefore not suitable for small children or pets. The 30 to 40 steps up to the cabin are steep and uneven; take extreme caution when loading gear in and out. No fires are allowed here at any time.

COST $40 per night. This money is used for maintenance and renovation of the structure.

RESERVATIONS The maximum stay is five consecutive nights. Call the toll-free National Recreation Reservation Service (1-877-444-6777) or make your reservations online at www.ReserveUSA.com.

HOW TO GET THERE To get there from Cave Junction, Oregon, travel south on Highway 199 for 6.4 miles to the Happy Camp Road. Turn left and

Bolan Mountain Lookout

travel 17.3 miles on Forest Road 46/Happy Camp Road to the junction with road 4812. Turn left and travel 4.1 miles to the junction of 4812-040, the road to Bolan Lake Campground. Turn left again, and travel 1.1 miles to road 535. Turn right and travel 1.6 miles to the Lookout. Road 535 is gated. Travel time is approximately 1.25 hours.

ELEVATION 6242 feet

WHAT IS PROVIDED The cabin is furnished with a table, two chairs, a single bed, footstool, broom, and fire extinguisher. An outhouse is nearby.

WHAT TO BRING Camping gear, including bedding and cooking supplies. There is no water available so bring as much as you'll need for drinking, cooking, and washing. Also bring along food, a flashlight, first-aid kit, toiletries, dishes, pots, pans, utensils, garbage bags, and a small camp cook stove and matches. There are no cooking facilities in the cabin.

HISTORY The original lookout was constructed on this site in 1917. The present structure has occupied this site since 1953.

AROUND YOU Bolan Campground and Lake. Also, the Bolan Lake Trail 1245. Port-Orford cedar root disease is a resource concern in southwest Oregon. The disease can be transported through mud or dirt on vehicles. You must wash you vehicle, including the undercarriage, before you enter National Forest lands. The area around the lookout contains sensitive plants. Plant collecting is not allowed in this location.

FOR MORE INFORMATION
Illinois Valley Ranger District
26568 Redwood Hwy
Cave Junction, OR 97523
(541) 592-4000
http://www.fs.fed.us/r6/rogue-siskiyou/recreation/cabins/index.shtml

"Nothing is more beautiful than the loveliness of the woods before sunrise."

George Washington Carver

34 Bald Knob Lookout

YOUR BEARINGS
15 miles south of Powers, Oregon.

AVAILABILITY Memorial Day weekend through the end of October, depending on weather conditions.

CAPACITY A maximum of four people.

DESCRIPTION This 16 x 16-foot flat top cabin sits atop a 20-foot tower.

COST $35 per night. This money is used for maintenance and renovation of the lookout.

RESERVATIONS Call the toll-free National Recreation Reservation Service (1-877-444-6777) or, make your reservations online at www.ReserveUSA.com.

HOW TO GET THERE The Lookout can be reached by driving south from the Powers Ranger District office on highway 242 through the town of Powers to the Forest boundary. Continue on Forest Service Road 33 along the South Fork of the Coquille River for approximately 11.5 miles to the junction of road 3348. Travel up road 3348 approximately 2 miles to the junction of road 5520. Turning right, the pavement ends. Take road 5520 for two miles, then turn right on road 5520-020 and follow this spur road approximately 2 miles until you reach a gate. Go through the gate and continue through a second gate until you arrive at the end of the lookout road.

ELEVATION 3630 feet

WHAT TO BRING Camping equipment, including bedding, and cooking supplies. There is no water at the site, so bring as much as you need for drinking, cooking, and washing.

WHAT IS PROVIDED The lookout is equipped with propane stove, heater, refrigerator, and lights. There is also a small table with chairs and a single bed. There is an outhouse located approximately 100 feet from the tower.

AROUND YOU At the Bald Knob Lookout, you are sure to enjoy a spectacular view overlooking Eden Valley, the Rogue River, and the forests beyond.

FOR MORE INFORMATION
Powers Ranger District
42861 Highway 242
Powers OR 97466
(541) 439-6200
http://www.fs.fed.us/r6/rogu
siskiyou/recreation/cabins
/bald-knob.shtml

Bald Knob Lookout

————————— —————————

> *"Like music and art, love of nature is a common language that can transcend political or social boundaries."*
>
> Jimmy Carter

35 Onion Mountain Lookout

YOUR BEARINGS
15 miles west of Grants Pass, Oregon

AVAILABILITY Available from May through October, depending on weather conditions.

CAPACITY A maximum of four people.

DESCRIPTION Onion Mountain is 14 x 14 feet, located 12 feet above the ground.

COST $40 per night. This money is used for maintenance and renovation of the lookout.

RESERVATIONS Call the toll-free National Recreation Reservation Service (1-877-444-6777) or make your reservations online at www.ReserveUSA.com.

HOW TO GET THERE From Grants Pass, Oregon, travel Highway 199 south to Riverbanks Road (milepost 7—just past the Applegate River) and turn right. Proceed on Riverbanks Road, 5.5 miles to Shan Creek Road and turn left. Proceed 8 miles on this gravel road to Forest Road 2509 and turn right. Proceed 0.75 mile to the Onion Mountain Gate. Alternate route: At milepost 15 of Highway 199, take Forest Road 25, 12 miles to Forest Road 2509 (Onion Mountain Road) and turn right. Proceed about 2.5 miles to the Onion Mountain gate.

ELEVATION 4438 feet

WHAT IS PROVIDED The Lookout has a vault toilet, gas stove, refrigerator, and a bed without a mattress. There is no drinking water so you will need to bring your own.

WHAT TO BRING Camping equipment, including bedding and cooking supplies. There is no water at the site, so bring as much as you need for drinking, cooking, and washing.

HISTORY Onion Mountain Lookout was built in 1916 and replaced with this structure in 1952.

Onion Mountain Lookout

Along with Dutchman Peak Lookout, it served as a primary lookout for this portion of the Rogue Valley.

AROUND YOU Onion Mountain offers spectacular views of mountainous southwest Oregon. At night, the twinkling lights of Grants Pass can be seen in the distance, along with a sky full of stars.

FOR MORE INFORMATION
Galice Ranger District
26568 Redwood Hwy
Cave Junction, OR 97523
(541) 471-6500
http://www.fs.fed.us/r6/
roguesiskiyou/recreation/
cabins/onion-mt.shtml

"The earth laughs in flowers."

E.E. Cummings

36 Imnaha Cabin

YOUR BEARINGS
22 miles northeast of Butte Falls, Oregon.

AVAILABILITY Year-round. Wheeled-vehicle access usually is possible only from the late spring through the early fall, so it offers a true winter recreation adventure to reach the cabin during snow season.

CAPACITY Six people maximum.

DESCRIPTION A cozy cabin in the forest with pine paneling and a lava rock fireplace. It is located adjacent to a small campground built in the 1930s during the Civilian Conservation Corps era.

COST $40 per night for the first two nights; $25 per night thereafter.

RESERVATIONS Reservations can be made for up to seven consecutive nights. Call the toll-free National Recreation Reservation Service (1-877-444-6777) or make your reservations online at www.ReserveUSA.com.

HOW TO GET THERE The cabin is reached by driving east from Butte Falls on County Road 821 (the Butte Falls/Fish Lake Highway). From County Road 821, less than a mile out of town, turn left and travel north on County Road 992 (the Butte Falls/Prospect Highway). Travel 8 miles on County Road 992 until you reach Forest Service Road 34. Turn right (northeast) and travel about 8 more miles on Forest Service Road 34 until you reach its junction with Forest Service Road 37.

Continue north-northeast on Road 37 for another 4.5 miles until you reach the Imnaha Campground turn-off. Imnaha Campground is located just a few hundred feet southeast down this road. Continuing through the Campground you will find Imnaha Cabin.

From the north, through the town of Prospect, Oregon, stay on the Butte Falls/Prospect Highway, County Road 992, for about 2.5 miles to Forest Service Road 37. Turn left (east) on Road 37 and continue on this road until you reach the entrance sign to Imnaha Campground. This is also the entrance to Imnaha Cabin.

ELEVATION 3800 feet

WHAT IS PROVIDED The cabin has one bedroom furnished with a full size bed and two dressers, a kitchen with a table, three chairs, propane-powered cook stove, range, lantern, and refrigerator. The living room is equipped with a fireplace, gas heater, coffee table, small futon couch, and chair (each with a fold-out bed). The cabin has potable water, a toilet and shower (available for summer use only) but no electricity. A mop, broom, bucket, snow-shovel, and fire extinguisher are also provided. Firewood is stacked in the garage adjacent to the cabin (splitting maul provided), but there is no guarantee that a supply will always be available for your stay.

WHAT TO BRING Camping equipment, including bedding and cooking supplies. In wintertime (November to April), there is no water at the site, so bring as much as you need for drinking, cooking, and washing this time of year. Bring basic cookware, dishes and utensils, flashlight, first-aid kit, matches, warm sleeping bags and pads, garbage bags to pack out trash, toilet articles, and other personal gear.

Imnaha Cabin

HISTORY The Guard Station cabin at Imnaha Springs was built in the 1930s, replacing a one-room Forest Service "shack" built there almost twenty years earlier. The cabin, built by the Civilian Conservation Corps during the Great Depression, is listed on the National Register of Historic Places. This small, rustic-style cottage is considered to be an outstanding example of CCC construction in the Pacific Northwest. The cabin is located next to the Imnaha Campground, also created by the CCC. The Butte Falls Ranger District used the cabin as a fire-watch or "guard" station through the late 1960s. Since the 1980s, Forest Service volunteer campground hosts have occupied the cabin most summers until it was added to the recreation rental program.

AROUND YOU Imnaha Guard Station is located in the southwest portion of Oregon's magnificent volcanic Cascade Range situated in the depths of old growth forest. Attractions such as Imnaha Springs and the "Big Fir Tree" are in the immediate vicinity for you to enjoy.

FOR MORE INFORMATION
Butte Falls Ranger District
800 Laurel Avenue
P.O. Box 227
Prospect, Oregon 97522
(541) 865-2700
http://www.fs.fed.us/r6/rogue-siskiyou/contact/butte.shtml

"Climb the mountains and get their good tidings. Nature's peace will flow into you as sunshine flows into trees. The winds will blow their own freshness into you, and the storms their energy, while cares will drop off like autumn leaves."

John Muir

37 Willow Prairie Cabin

YOUR BEARINGS
40 miles east of Medford, Oregon

AVAILABILITY Year-round. There is a big difference between summer and winter seasons at Willow Prairie. Vehicle access in winter is subject to weather conditions. Wintertime parking is available along Highway 140 with an Oregon State Parks Sno-Park pass. You may purchase the pass in advance at Department of Motor Vehicles offices. The Forest Service is not selling the passes, so be sure you have one before you leave town. You may have to ski, snowshoe, or snowmobile over snow the last 1 to 6 miles to access the cabin.

CAPACITY Four people maximum.

DESCRIPTION If you have ever dreamed of returning to the "Old West" and living the life of a cowboy, or holing up in a cabin overnight and riding the trails without a care, just you and your horse, then we have the perfect place for you. The Butte Falls Ranger District is offering the Willow Prairie Cabin as a year-round rental for campers, hikers, and summer and winter sports enthusiasts who want a roof over their head for the evening. It is a one-room cabin with two shutter style windows (no glass) and a front door. Willow Prairie Cabin is list on the National Register of Historic Places.

COST $15 per night. Rental fees are used for maintenance of the historic cabin.

RESERVATIONS The minimum stay is one night and the maximum is seven consecutive nights. Call the toll-free National Recreation Reservation Service (1-877-444-6777) or make your reservations online at www.ReserveUSA.com.

HOW TO GET THERE From the town of Butte Falls, travel County Road 821 (Butte Falls/Fish Lake Highway) and drive approximately 17 miles southeast to Forest Service Road 3738. If you are entering the Butte Falls Ranger District from Highway 140, turn north on County Road 821 from Highway 140 and drive approximately 2 miles northwest to Forest Service Road 3738. Turn west on Road 3738 and continue 1.3 miles to where 3738 intersects Forest Service road 3735. At this point, you have two choices:

If you are pulling a trailer, or driving a vehicle with low clearance, turn left and travel 0.25 mile to the Willow Prairie Campground overflow parking area. Here is where you can unload horses and park the horse trailer or vehicle during your stay.

If you are not pulling a trailer and have a high-clearance vehicle, continue due west across the intersection, off the main road, and onto a little dirt road that ambles through the trees. At the next junction, turn left. The cabin should be in sight at this point. Continue on to the designated loading/unloading area located within 200 feet of the cabin.

ELEVATION 4300 feet

WHAT IS PROVIDED The cabin has a wood stove, and some rustic furniture, as well as a couple of sleeping cots. There is counter space and places to hang lanterns. Firewood is provided at times, however you are encouraged to bring your own, or an alternative heat source. A splitting maul is provided. You will have the luxury of potable water just 400 feet from the cabin and livestock water just 200 feet from the cabin IN SUMMER MONTHS ONLY. There are four stock corrals (12 x 12 feet in size) located 100 feet from the cabin. Firewood is also provided, but the District cannot guarantee a supply, so recommends you bring an alternate source of heat. A splitting maul and wheelbarrow are on site as well as an outhouse 600 feet from the cabin.

WHAT TO BRING Camping equipment, including bedding and cooking supplies. Bring a camp stove, all cookware, dishes and utensils, warm sleeping bags and pads, lanterns, matches and flashlights. Bring a first-aid kit, garbage bags to haul out your trash, and any personal gear. There is no water at the site during winter, so bring as much as you need for drinking, cooking, and washing.

HISTORY In 1924, a road crew constructing the Butte Falls/Fish Lake Highway built the cabin to use as housing while they completed their task. Willow Prairie was a very remote area in those days, so the crew could not travel to their homes at the end of the day. Over the years the Forest Service preserved the cabin, and built the Willow Prairie Campground adjacent to the cabin site. Willow Prairie Cabin is now listed on the National Register of Historic Places. In 1991 the campground was converted to a horse camp. The cabin is considered the premium site available.

AROUND YOU Willow Prairie Cabin is adjacent to the Willow Prairie Horse Camp, and is surrounded by nineteen-plus miles of horse trails. There are corrals and a water trough for up to four horses.

FOR MORE INFORMATION
Butte Falls Ranger District
47201 Highway 62
Prospect, Oregon 97536-9724
(541) 865-2700
http://www.fs.fed.us/r6/rogue-siskiyou/recreation/cabins/
willowprairie.shtml

Willow Prairie Cabin

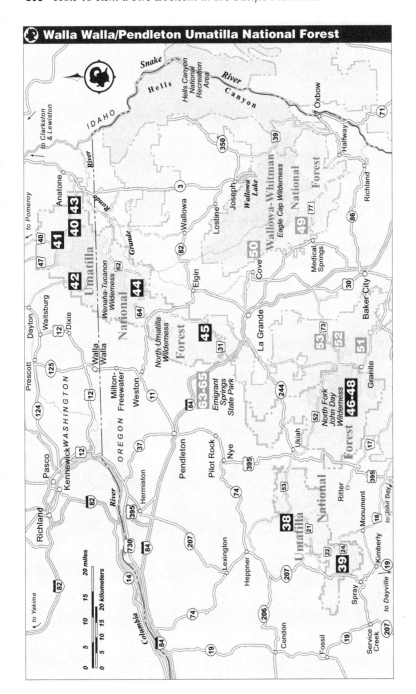

Walla Walla/Pendleton Umatilla National Forest

Umatilla National Forest

> *"I am no more lonely than a single mullen or a dande-lion in a pasture, or a bean leaf, or sorree, or a horsefly, or a bumblebee."*

Henry David Thoreau, *Walden*

38 Ditch Creek Guard Station

YOUR BEARINGS

25 miles west of Ukiah
27 miles southeast of Heppner, Oregon
75 miles southwest of Pendleton
75 miles west of La Grande
110 miles northwest of John Day

AVAILABILITY Year-round. Automobile access to the cabin runs from mid-May to mid-November. Winter use will require alternate transportation such as skis, snowshoes, or snowmobiles.

Ditch Creek Guard Station

CAPACITY Six people maximum.

DESCRIPTION The cabin is a one-story building containing a bedroom, living room, bathroom with shower, and kitchen with nook. It is not accessible to wheelchairs due to narrow doors and hallways.

COST $40 per night

RESERVATIONS Call the toll-free National Recreation Reservation Service (1-877-444-6777) or make your reservations online at www.ReserveUSA.com.

HOW TO GET THERE From Heppner, Oregon, travel one mile south toward the Willow Creek Reservoir on Willow Creek Road. Turn left (east) onto the Blue Mountain Scenic Byway (Highway 678—which becomes Forest Road 53 at the National Forest boundary). Continue on Road 53 to its junction with Forest Road 21, a distance of four miles. (It is 21 miles from the town of Heppner to Forest Road 21). Turn right on Road 21 (gravel), and travel three miles south. The Guard Station is on a small hill on the west side of the road, up a short drive.

From Pendleton take Highway 395 south for 47 miles to Highway 53 West—about a mile or so west of Ukiah, Oregon. From Ukiah take County Road 244 west (it becomes Forest Road 53) for 22 miles to Forest Road 21. Turn left (south) on Road 21 and travel three miles on gravel to the Guard Station.

SAFETY CONSIDERATIONS The portions of Willow Creek Road and Forest Road 21 closest to the Guard Station are not plowed in the winter, so the nearest parking from October through May, depending on snow accumulation, could be up to 5.5 miles away, at Cutsforth Park. Contact the Heppner Ranger District for current road and weather information prior to your visit.

ELEVATION 4800 feet

WHAT IS PROVIDED There are two bunk beds and a dresser in the bedroom and a table with four chairs, and two easy chairs and a heating stove in the living room. The kitchen has a refrigerator, cook stove, fire extinguisher, cookware, silverware, and dishes. The nook has two additional chairs and a small table. There is a water heater and a utility closet in the entrance area with a mop, broom, and cleaning supplies. All appliances and lighting are propane, which is provided by the Forest Service.

Outside, there is a picnic table, fire pit, and a 20 x 20-foot horse corral for use by cabin renters. The fire pit may only be used during acceptable fire danger levels (inquire at the District Office prior to arrival).

WHAT TO BRING Bring potable water for cooking, drinking, and washing as there is NO WATER available at this cabin. Bring camping supplies as well as garbage bags (pack it in, pack it out), candles or a lantern for emergencies, first aid kit, sleeping bag/bedding, toiletries, washcloths and towels, dish soap, and bar soap.

HISTORY The building complex was built in 1934, and is a National Historic Landmark, exemplary of the architectural style used by the Civilian Conservation Corp during the 1930s in the Pacific Northwest. Ditch Creek Cabin has been open for rent since October of 1996.

AROUND YOU The Bald Mountain trail system can be reached from Coalmine Park, a 3-mile drive from the guard station. The Heppner Ranger District offers a wide variety of recreational opportunities that can be accessed from both Ditch Creek Guard Station and Tamarack Lookout. There are over 26 miles of trails that are available for hiking or horseback riding. Fishing opportunities exist in streams throughout the district as well as Penland Lake (electric motors only) and Bull Prairie Lake (no motors allowed).

FOR MORE INFORMATION
Heppner Ranger District
P.O. Box 7
Heppner, Oregon 97836
(541) 676-9187
http://www.fs.fed.us/r6/uma/recreation/cabins/hepcabins.shtml

"One touch of nature makes the whole world kin."

William Shakespeare

39 Tamarack Lookout Cabin

YOUR BEARINGS
43 miles south of Heppner, Oregon

AVAILABILITY Tamarack Lookout Cabin is available year-round. Automobile access to the cabin runs from mid-May through mid-November depending on the weather conditions. Winter use will require alternate transportation such as skis, snowshoes, or snowmobiles.

CAPACITY 4 people maximum.

DESCRIPTION The cabin is a one-room facility overlooking the John Day River basin, between Spray and Kimberly.

COST $25 per night.

RESERVATIONS Call the toll-free National Recreation Reservation Service (1-877-444-6777) or make your reservations online at www.ReserveUSA.com.

HOW TO GET THERE Tamarack Cabin is located approximately 43 miles south of Heppner, Oregon. From West I-84 take Highway 74 to Lexington/Heppner. Drive 45 miles through the towns of Ione and Lexington to Heppner. Continue south on Hwy 207 for 39 miles through Heppner, Ruggs, and Hardman, and past Anson Wright County Park to the junction of Highway 207 and Forest Service Road 24 (0.1 mile past the Bull Prairie Campground turnoff). Turn left (east) on Road 24 (gravel) and travel 6.5 miles to Forest Service Road 2407. Turn right (south) on Road 2407 and travel 1.5 miles to Forest Service Road 040. Travel 0.5 miles on Road 040 to the cabin. The cabin is on the right before you get to the Helispot.

From Ukiah take Forest Service Road 53, west. Cross Highway 395 and continue on Road 53 to its junction with Forest Service Road 21 (approximately 23 miles from Ukiah). Take a left (west) on Road 21 (gravel) and travel 31 miles past Ditch Creek Guard Station and Tupper Guard Station to Highway 207. Take a left (south) on Highway 207 and travel 6.5 miles to the junction of Highway 207 and Forest Service Road 24 (0.1 mile past the Bull Prairie Campground turnoff). Take a left (east) on Road 24 (gravel) and follow the directions above to the cabin.

From Central Oregon take Highway 207 (north), 3 miles east of Spray. Travel 10.5 miles to the junction of Highway 207 and Forest Service Road 24. Take a right (east) on Road 24 and follow the directions above to the cabin.

Tamarack Lookout Cabin

Forest Service Road 24 to the cabin is not plowed during the winter; therefore, access to the cabin may be limited. A pickup with high clearance is recommended 12 months out of the year. Contact the Heppner Ranger District for information regarding current road conditions.

ELEVATION 4979 feet

WHAT IS PROVIDED The cabin is furnished with a cook stove, cookware, silverware, dishes, a heating stove, two bunk beds, and an outdoor restroom. All appliances and lighting are propane. The Forest Service provides propane.

WHAT TO BRING Bring potable water for cooking, drinking, and washing as there is NO WATER available at this cabin. Bring camping supplies as well as garbage bags (pack it in, pack it out), candles or a lantern for emergencies, first aid kit, sleeping bag/bedding, toiletries, washcloths and towels, dish soap, and bar soap.

HISTORY Tamarack Lookout Cabin has been open for rent since May of 2000. Originally, it was housing for Forest Service personnel using the lookout for fire detection. The original cabin was built in 1934 and destroyed by an accidental fire in 1966. A garage/utility shed was then converted to the existing cabin.

AROUND YOU The Heppner Ranger District offers a wide variety of recreational opportunities that can be accessed from both Ditch Creek Guard Station and Tamarack Lookout. There are over 26 miles of trails that are available for hiking or horseback riding. Fishing opportunities exist in streams throughout the district as well as Penland Lake (electric motors only) and Bull Prairie Lake (no motors allowed).

FOR MORE INFORMATION
Heppner Ranger District
P.O. Box 7
Heppner, Oregon 97836
(541) 676-9187
http://www.fs.fed.us/r6/uma/recreation/cabins/hepcabins.shtml#ditch

> *"The golden moments in the stream of life rush past us, and we see nothing but sand; the angels come to visit us, and we only know them when they are gone."*
>
> George Eliot

40 Clearwater Lookout Cabin

YOUR BEARINGS

23 miles southeast of Pomeroy, Washington
60 miles northeast of Walla Walla, Washington
90 miles west of Lewiston, Idaho
100 miles northeast of Pendleton, Oregon
150 miles south of Spokane, Washington

AVAILABILITY Year-round. Automobile access to the site is typically possible from June 1 to November 1. Winter use will require alternate transportation such as skis, snowshoes, or snowmobile.

CAPACITY Four people maximum.

DESCRIPTION Single-story wood frame structure with 360 square feet of floor space.

COST $25 per night.

RESERVATIONS Call the toll-free National Recreation Reservation Service (1-877-444-6777) or make your reservations online at www.ReserveUSA.com.

Clearwater Lookout Cabin

HOW TO GET THERE Traveling through Pomeroy, Washington, on Highway 12 East (Main Street), you will notice toward the end of town a sign that reads UMATILLA NATIONAL FOREST 15 MILES. Follow this by turning right. This is 15th Street and becomes, in time, Road 128, Road 107, and Road 40—but this is all academic since most of these roads are not signed.

However, by following 15th Street south for 23 miles you will eventually reach the cabin. It is on the right. The road is paved to the National Forest boundary—about the first 15 miles. It is gravel thereafter but fairly well-maintained. The route is open to automobiles from about June 1 to November 1. Winter use may require travel by skis or snowshoes. Consult the District Office regarding current road and snow conditions prior to your departure.

ELEVATION 5600 feet

WHAT IS PROVIDED Propane cook stove, heater, light, and fridge, a chest of drawers, desk, table, chairs, and closet. The bedroom sleeps four, with two metal-framed single beds and a metal-framed double bunk.

The cabin is in need of the kind of loving attention that perhaps some local volunteers, in cooperation with the Forest Service, will give. The grounds are bereft of trees or shade, leaving the cabin itself exposed and looking somewhat bedraggled. It has only a very limited view and, despite its name, has no water, clear or otherwise.

WHAT TO BRING Bring potable water for cooking, drinking, and washing as there is NO WATER available at this cabin. Bring camping supplies as well as garbage bags (pack it in, pack it out), candles or a lantern for emergencies, first aid kit, sleeping bag/bedding, toiletries, washcloths and towels, dish soap, and bar soap.

HISTORY The cabin was built in 1935 as a residence for the Clearwater Lookout guard. It still serves that purpose occasionally.

AROUND YOU Scenic drive along breaks of the Tucannon River (Sunset Point). Horse and/or hiking trail into Tucannon River offers great seasonal opportunities for wild mushroom and berry picking. Also enjoy wildlife viewing, and in winter, snowmobiling and cross-country skiing on groomed trails.

FOR MORE INFORMATION
Pomeroy Ranger District
71 West Main
Pomeroy, Washington 99347
(509) 843-1891
http://www.fs.fed.us/r6/uma/recreation/cabins/pomcabins.shtml

"The worse I get along with people the more I learn to have faith in Nature and concentrate on her."

Vincent Van Gogh

41 Clearwater Big House Cabin

YOUR BEARINGS This site is located approximately 23 miles south of Pomeroy, Washington on the Umatilla National Forest.

AVAILABILITY Year-round. Automobile access to the site is typically possible from June 1 to November 1. Winter use will require alternate transportation such as skis, snowshoes, or snowmobile.

CAPACITY 10 people maximum.

DESCRIPTION This is a two-story cabin, built in 1934. The first floor is 868 square feet and the second floor is 336 square feet. It has three bedrooms, a living room, kitchen, and a bathroom with hot shower.

COST $40 to $60 per night, depending on number of occupants. Water available during summer months.

RESERVATIONS Call the toll-free National Recreation Reservation Service (1-877-444-6777) or make your reservations online at www.ReserveUSA.com.

HOW TO GET THERE From Pomeroy, Washington, take 15th Street south (which becomes County Mountain Road, or the old Highway 128) for 15 miles to the National Forest boundary. Continue on Forest Service Road 40 for nine miles to Clearwater Junction. Turn left onto Forest Service Road 42. Travel 0.25 mile and turn right into the Clearwater Guard Station area.

ELEVATION 5600 feet

WHAT IS PROVIDED Water is available on site from June to October. Otherwise, bring your own. Four double beds, two single beds, some cooking dishes and utensils, fire extinguisher, and smoke detector are provided. Also you will find a propane heater, cook stove and small refrigerator. There is an indoor flush toilet and shower during the summer season and an outhouse for winter use—as water is turned off at this time.

WHAT TO BRING Bring potable water for cooking, drinking, and washing as there is NO WATER available at this cabin except during summer months. Bring camping supplies as well as garbage bags (pack it in, pack it out), candles or a lantern for emergencies, first aid kit, sleeping bag/bedding, toiletries, washcloths and towels, dish soap, and bar soap.

HISTORY Clearwater was originally the site of an old trapper cabin, which was converted to a Ranger Station in 1928. The cabin now standing was built in 1934, remodeled in 1965, and remodeled again in 1997.

AROUND YOU Scenic drive along breaks of the Tucannon River (Sunset Point). Horse and/or hiking trail into Tucannon River offers great seasonal opportunities for wild mushroom and berry picking. Also enjoy wildlife viewing, and in winter, snowmobiling and cross-country skiing on groomed trails.

FOR MORE INFORMATION
Pomeroy Ranger District
71 West Main
Pomeroy, Washington 99347
(509) 843-1891
http://www.fs.fed.us/r6/uma/recreation/cabins/pomcabins.shtml

"The bluebird carries the sky on his back."
Henry David Thoreau, *Journal*, April 3, 1852

42 Godman Guard Station

YOUR BEARINGS
28 miles southeast of Dayton, Washington
60 miles east of Walla Walla Washington
95 miles southwest of Lewiston, Idaho (via Dayton)
100 miles northeast of Pendleton, Oregon
155 miles south of Spokane, Washington

AVAILABILITY Year-round. Automobile access to the site is typically possible from June 1 to November 1. Winter use will require alternate transportation such as skis, snowshoes, or snowmobile.

CAPACITY Eight people maximum.

DESCRIPTION A nicely secluded 2-story guard station with living room, kitchen, bathroom, and two bedrooms. There is a smaller house (with woodstove) adjacent to the guard station; it is available to skiers and snowshoers as a free day-use warming shelter.

COST $40 to $60 depending on the number of occupants.

RESERVATIONS Call the toll-free National Recreation Reservation Service (1-877-444-6777) or make your reservations online at www.ReserveUSA.com.

HOW TO GET THERE The route is open to motor vehicles from about June 1 to November 1. Winter use may require travel by skis or snowshoes.

Consult the District Office regarding current road and snow conditions prior to your departure.

Getting to this place can be as confusing as finding your way around the Internet. The Forest Service directions make getting there seem simple—except that not one of the county roads is signed, which renders those directions useless, as we found, having gotten lost several times. Here, whenever possible, we will use the road and street names that are signed, rather than guiding you by their map numbers.

From Main Street of Dayton, Washington—Highway 12 East—turn right onto 4th Street. Follow 4th Street for about 0.5 mile and turn left onto Eckler Street—not Eckler Mountain Road. Eckler Street becomes East Mustard Street, which leads to Skyline Drive. This is the road that goes to the National Forest and eventually becomes Forest Road 46, but not before you drive through about 18 miles of wheat fields. It is about 28 miles to the Godman Guard Station.

Just before the Godman Campground and a horse barn, turn left onto Forest Road 4608—the guard station is a few hundred yards up this road.

ELEVATION 5600 feet

WHAT IS PROVIDED Indoor plumbing—water is available during summer months, though in winter the water is turned off to prevent pipe-freeze. Check with the Ranger District on the status of available water prior to your stay. If the system is off, bring your own drinking water, or have the means to treat the local supply.

The living room has propane lights, woodstove, couch, chest of drawers, a nice table, and a linoleum floor. The kitchen has a propane

Godman Guard Station

cook stove and fridge, and a sink. The downstairs bedroom has a wooden floor and three single metal-framed beds with less-than-inviting mattresses. The upstairs bedroom has two double beds and one single bed.

WHAT TO BRING Bring potable water for cooking, drinking, and washing when water is not available at this cabin. Bring camping supplies as well as garbage bags (pack it in, pack it out), candles or a lantern for emergencies, first aid kit, sleeping bag/bedding, toiletries, washcloths and towels, dish soap, and bar soap.

HISTORY The Godman region has been used by area residents for summer camps and "tent homes" since the early 1900s. Construction of the guard station (the big house) began in 1933 when a Civilian Conservation Corps camp was located in the area.

AROUND YOU The guard station is nicely secluded down in a hollow. Considering that there is a horse barn on the brow of the hill between the cabin and the wilderness, and a campground across the road from the horse barn, this seclusion is a blessing. A lovely creek runs through the backyard.

You are on the very rim of the Wenaha-Tucannon Wilderness portion of the Blue Mountains. The Godman Trail (3138) will lead you as deeply into it as you want to go.

FOR MORE INFORMATION
Pomeroy Ranger District
71 West Main
Pomeroy, Washington 99347
(509) 843-1891
http://www.fs.fed.us/r6/uma/recreation/cabins/pomcabins.shtml

"It appeared to be the most beautiful valley I had ever looked upon...thousands of ponies grazing, and Indians driving in all directions."

John Johnson, July 1851,
on seeing the Grande Ronde Valley

43 Wenatchee Guard Station

YOUR BEARINGS
40 miles southeast of Pomeroy, WA
70 miles southwest of Lewiston, ID (via Pomeroy)
105 miles northeast of Walla Walla, WA
145 miles northeast of Pendleton, OR
180 miles south of Spokane, WA

AVAILABILITY Year-round. Automobile access to the site is typically possible from June 1 to November 1. Winter use will require alternate transportation such as skis, snowshoes, or snowmobile.

CAPACITY Four people maximum, though two would be more comfortable. Good for families.

DESCRIPTION One-story cabin with living room, bedroom and small kitchen. Secluded and comfortable, with extraordinary views.

COST $30 per night.

RESERVATIONS Call the toll-free National Recreation Reservation Service (1-877-444-6777) or make your reservations online at www.ReserveUSA.com.

HOW TO GET THERE The route is open to motor vehicles from about June 1 to November 1. Winter use may require travel by skis or snowshoes. Consult the District Office regarding current road and snow conditions prior to your departure.

Traveling through Pomeroy, Washington, on Highway 12 East (Main Street), you will notice toward the end of town a sign that reads UMATILLA NATIONAL FOREST 15. Follow this by turning right. This is 15th Street which, over the next 15 miles, becomes, respectively, Roads 128, 107, and Forest Road 40 at the National Forest boundary. Here its surface changes to fairly well-maintained gravel. Continue on Road 40 another 16 miles to where it becomes Forest Road 44. After another 3.5 miles continue straight ahead—off Forest Road 44 and onto Forest Road 43. These roads are well signed. Go east on Road 43 for another

Wenatchee Guard Station

three miles. The Guard Station is on a hill on the left side of the road. It is clearly visible.

But even before reaching the Guard Station you will be treated to astonishing vistas of Wenatchee Creek Canyon, Grande Ronde Valley, Wenaha-Tucannon Wilderness, and more.

ELEVATION 6050 feet

WHAT IS PROVIDED Propane heat, lights, cook stove, and fridge. The small kitchen has a sink, but no running water. The bedroom has two single beds, and the living room/dining room also has a single bed.

WHAT TO BRING Bring potable water for cooking, drinking, and washing as there is NO WATER available at this cabin. Bring camping supplies as well as garbage bags (pack it in, pack it out), candles or a lantern for emergencies, first aid kit, sleeping bag/bedding, toiletries, washcloths and towels, dish soap, and bar soap.

SETTING This historic guard station has a very cozy and comfortable ambience. It is beautifully proportioned and exquisitely secluded atop a ledge that looks into eternity.

HISTORY Built in 1933 by Civilian Conservation Corps enrollees stationed in the District.

AROUND YOU Beside the cabin, off Forest Road 43, is the trailhead for the Ranger Creek Trail (3137), which follows Ranger Creek to the Menatchee Creek, and follows that all the way to the Grande Ronde Valley.

The simplest way to reach Wenaha-Tucannon Wilderness is to go west from the cabin, on Forest Road 43, to Misery Spring Campground. At the campground turn left onto Forest Road 4030 and travel one mile to Kelly Camp Trailhead (3120).

Enjoy a scenic drive along Wenatchee Creek Canyon. Then, leave the car and travel the horse and/or hiker trail into Wenatchee Creek. In winter, experience snowshoeing and cross-country skiing on groomed trails.

FOR MORE INFORMATION
Pomeroy Ranger District
71 West Main
Pomeroy, Washington 99347
(509) 843-1891
http://www.fs.fed.us/r6/uma/recreation/cabins/pomcabins.shtml

> *"Life consists with wilderness. The most alive is the*
> *wildest. Not yet subdued to man, its presence refreshes him."*
>
> Henry David Thoreau, 1862

44 Fry Meadow Guard Station

YOUR BEARINGS

25 miles north of Elgin
50 miles northeast of La Grande
80 miles northwest of Enterprise
90 miles north of Baker City
100 miles east of Pendleton

AVAILABILITY All year. Automobile access to the site runs from June 1 to November 1. Winter use will require alternate transportation such as skis, snowshoes, or snowmobile.

CAPACITY Four people maximum. Ideal for families.

DESCRIPTION Small cabin with bedroom, living room, and kitchen. No stove or heater.

COST $25 per night.

RESERVATIONS Call the toll-free National Recreation Reservation Service (1-877-444-6777) or make your reservations online at www.ReserveUSA.com.

Fry Meadow Guard Station

HOW TO GET THERE The route is open to vehicular travel from about May 1 to December 1. Winter use may require you to travel by skis or snowshoes. Consult the District Office regarding current road and snow conditions prior to your departure.

The Forest Service directions make getting there seem simple—except that most of the roads are not signed, which renders those directions useless, as we found, having gotten lost several times. Here, whenever possible, we will use the road and street names that are signed, rather than guiding you by their map numbers.

From La Grande, take Highway 82 northeast 20 miles to the town of Elgin. This is where it gets sticky. At the main crossroads in the town of Elgin turn left. After about one mile, turn right. Follow the signs for LOOKINGGLASS FISH HATCHERY and PALMER JUNCTION via Middle Road and Gordon Creek Road for about 20 miles, to Palmer Junction. These roads are numbered on the map as County Road 42, but are not signed as such.

Continue just a few hundred yards past Palmer Junction on Road 42 (which is signed Moses Creek Lane—do not take Lookingglass Road) until you come to Lookout Mountain Road (Forest Road 43). Turn left here and continue on this poorly maintained, winding, steep road for eight miles—it becomes Forest Road 6231. You will finally see a sign for Fry Meadow. Turn left at this sign; this is Forest Road 6235. The cabin is on your left about 100 yards after the turn, set at the sylvan corner of a lovely meadow.

A longer route, but with a slightly better road, is to follow the BOWMAN LOOP and JUBILEE LAKE signs from Road 42 two miles west of Palmer Junction. Go north on Forest Road 63 (unmarked) for five miles to Forest Road 62. Turn right (northeast) onto Road 62, and continue four miles to Forest Road 6235. Turn right onto Road 6235. The cabin is a mile ahead on the right, 100 yards from the junction of Road 6231.

ELEVATION 4138 feet

WHAT IS PROVIDED Fry Meadow Guard Station is furnished with a propane cooking stove, table and four chairs, four cots for sleeping bags, and outside toilet. No water available at the cabin.

WHAT TO BRING Bring potable water for cooking, drinking and washing as there is NO WATER available at this cabin. Bring camping supplies as well as garbage bags (pack it in, pack it out), candles or a lantern for emergencies, first aid kit, sleeping bag/bedding, toiletries, washcloths and towels, dish soap, and bar soap.

SETTING The cabin, surrounded by fine old trees, peacefully overlooks a meadow that was luscious with wildflowers the day we were there; and that evening, as we sat on the picnic table by the fire ring when the birds began their evening song with full-throated ease, the meadow became Keats' "melodious plot of beechen green, and shadows numberless. "

HISTORY Fry Meadow Guard Station is south of Wenaha-Tucannon Wilderness and west of the Wild and Scenic Grande Ronde River. The Grande Ronde Valley was named by a French fur-trapper for its circular shape. From 1843 on, hundreds of thousands of emigrants passed through here on their way to the Willamette Valley.

In better days—for Native Americans, anyway—the Nez Perce, Cayuse, Umatilla, Bannock, Yakima, and Walla Walla tribes shared the Grande Ronde Valley and its hot springs and food in all its natural abundance.

John C. Fremont, when he saw this valley in October 1843, wrote in his journal, "It is a place—one of the few we have seen in our journey so far—where a farmer would delight to establish himself, if he were content to live in the seclusion it imposes...it may in time, form a superb country."

Fry Meadow was first established as a Forest Service Ranger Station sometime before 1908 for what was then called Wenaha National Forest. The Guard Station was built in the early 1930s by the Civilian Conservation Corps; it is a classic example of their Depression Era architectural styling and construction.

Lookingglass Fish Hatchery gets its interesting name from a Nez Perce leader called Apash-wa-hay-ikt, but called Chief Looking Glass by Europeans because he often carried a hand-mirror with him.

AROUND YOU The 200 miles of trails in Wenaha-Tucannon Wilderness can be reached by following either Forest Roads 6231 north or 6235 northwest to Forest Road 62. Go north on Road 62 to its junction with Forest Road 6413. Turn left onto Road 6413, and then right onto Road 6415 to Trail 3236 and the wilderness entry. In addition, the entire area around Fry Meadow is a maze of logging roads. All invite a saunter.

The Fry Meadow Guard Station is located just south of the Wenaha-Tucannon Wilderness, and west of the wild and scenic Grande Ronde River. The area offers great seasonal opportunities for wild mushroom and berry picking.

FOR MORE INFORMATION
Walla Walla Ranger District
1415 West Rose St.
Walla Walla, Washington 99362
(509) 522-6290
http://www.fs.fed.us/r6/uma/recreation/cabins/wwcabins.shtml

"I frequently met old acquaintances, in the trees and flowers, and was not a little delighted. Indeed I do not know as I was ever so much affected with any scenery in my life... "

From the diary of Narcissa Whitman,
pioneer to this area, 1836

45 Summit Guard Station Bunkhouse

YOUR BEARINGS

35 miles north of La Grande
41 miles southeast of Pendleton
75 miles north of Baker City
90 miles south of Walla Walla

AVAILABILITY Year-round. Automobile access to the site runs from June 1 to November 1. Winter use will require alternate transportation such as skis, snowshoes, or snowmobile.

CAPACITY Four people maximum. Good for families.

DESCRIPTION 24 x 15-foot one-room bunkhouse with a very low ceiling. In need of some Forest Service T.L.C., but with panoramic views.

COST $35 per night.

Summit Guard Station Bunkhouse

RESERVATIONS Call the toll-free National Recreation Reservation Service (1-877-444-6777) or make your reservations online at www.ReserveUSA.com.

HOW TO GET THERE The route is open to vehicular travel from about May 1 to December 1. Winter use may require you to travel by skis or snowshoes. Consult the District Office regarding current road and snow conditions prior to your departure.

From Pendleton travel southeast on Interstate 84 for about 38 miles and take the SUMMIT ROAD—MT. EMILY exit. Go northeast on Summit Road (Forest Road 31), which is gravel, for 12 miles to its junction with Forest Road 3113. Turn left here; the bunkhouse is a mile ahead on the left. Note that Summit Guard Station, the first structure on the left, is not for rent. The Bunkhouse is the only cabin here available for overnight guests.

ELEVATION 4780 feet

WHAT IS PROVIDED The bunkhouse is furnished with propane heater, range, table and four chairs, four bed frames, and outside toilet. No potable water source available at the site.

WHAT TO BRING Bring potable water for cooking, drinking, and washing as there is NO WATER available at this cabin. Bring camping supplies as well as garbage bags (pack it in, pack it out), candles or a lantern for emergencies, first aid kit, sleeping bag/bedding, toiletries, washcloths and towels, dish soap, and bar soap.

HISTORY The Summit Ranger Station was established here sometime before 1908 as an administrative site for what used to be called Wenaha National Forest. The original cabin was replaced with a residence built by the Civilian Conservation Corps in 1934. The Guard Station is still used by Forest Service fire crews. The bunkhouse itself was built in the 1970s and is purely utilitarian, entirely lacking the charm and grace of the work done in earlier times, but, from its position atop Drumhill Ridge, it does preside over a grand and expansive view.

AROUND YOU Magnificent views overlooking sections of the Grande Ronde Valley, with snow-capped peaks in the distance. On the way up Forest Road 31 you will find an interpretive sign a short distance before Forest Road 3109, showing where Marcus and Narcissa Whitman, with Reverend and Eliza Spalding, crossed the summit in 1836. Ms. Whitman and Ms. Spalding became the first European women to cross the continent traveling this route.

On graveled Forest Road 3109 stop at the Whitman Route Overlook for a sweeping vista of this rugged and remote terrain. The bunkhouse itself overlooks a chunk of the Blue Mountains that includes Sugarloaf, Spring, Green, and Wilbur mountains. In addition, it is surrounded by massive old-growth trees that provide day-long shade. There were deer prancing around much of the afternoon we spent there, and not a single car went by nor did we encounter anyone on our way to or from the cabin; though a coyote did eye us knowingly on the way back.

The Bear Creek Trail is within walking distance of the cabin, and travels through old-growth forest to the North Fork Meacham Creek, which it follows for 2.5 miles; then climbs 3.5 miles to the top of Thimbleberry Mountain.

FOR MORE INFORMATION
Walla Walla Ranger District
1415 West Rose St.
Walla Walla, Washington 99362
(509) 522-6290
http://www.fs.fed.us/r6/uma/recreation/cabins/wwcabins.shtml

"The idea of wilderness needs no defense. It only needs more defenders."

Edward Abbey

46 Miner's Retreat

YOUR BEARINGS
59 miles southeast of Ukiah, Oregon
40 miles west of Baker City, Oregon
5 miles west of Granite, Oregon

AVAILABILITY Year-round, however the cabin may be closed occasionally for administrative needs and maintenance. Access to motor vehicles is open during the late spring, summer, and early fall months. In winter, access is by over-snow transportation (skis, snowshoes or snowmobiles). During these months, vehicle parking is off-site. Check with the Ranger District for current weather and road conditions prior to your arrival.

CAPACITY A maximum of six adults, with sleeping accommodations for four. Dogs are welcome at the cabin provided the owner picks up after them. Be aware that the structure has D-Con (rodent poison) placed within its perimeters. If you allow pets to wander freely, please keep them from disturbing wildlife and vegetation.

DESCRIPTION This two-bedroom cabin has a kitchen, living room, and bathroom as well as a roomy front porch. It has wood siding, tin roofing, and a cement foundation. A concrete walkway leads to the front porch steps and an enclosed rear entry is located of the kitchen for back door access. It is on the National Register of Historic Places. It is the middle residence of the Fremont Powerhouse Complex. Smaller, one- and two-bedroom cabins are also located at this complex and are available to rent. (see chapters on Hilltop Hideaway and Congo Gulch rentals).

COST $50 per night. Winter rates start October 1st for $30 per night.

RESERVATIONS Call the toll-free National Recreation Reservation Service (1-877-444-6777) or make your reservations online at www.ReserveUSA.com. Reservations are limited to 14 consecutive nights during a 30-day period, from noon to noon.

HOW TO GET THERE From Ukiah, proceed on Camas Street in a southeast direction (it becomes County Road 1475 at the city limits) for approximately 6 miles. Here, at the National Forest boundary it becomes Forest Service Road 52. Continue on Forest Road 52 for 40 miles to the North Fork John Day Campground. At this location, Forest Service Road 52 becomes Forest Service Road 73. Continue on Road 73 for 8 miles to the junction of Forest Service Road 73 and forest Service Road 10. The town of Granite is on the left side of the road. Travel west on Forest Road 10 for 5 miles to the Fremont Powerhouse Complex. Miner's Retreat is the middle cabin in the Complex.

ELEVATION 4939 feet

WHAT IS PROVIDED During the summer and fall months, potable water is available on site, as well as the luxury of indoor plumbing. During the winter and early spring months, the plumbing is shut down. Water will need to be carried in during this time. An outhouse is on site.

Miner's Retreat

On a year-round basis the cabin is equipped with electric heat, light, refrigerator, stove/oven, beds, living room furniture, kitchen table, chairs, some kitchen gear (skillets, coffee pot, glasses, cups, dishes, silverware), and storage areas. Cleaning supplies are provided. Pack out your trash, please.

WHAT TO BRING Water during late fall, winter, and early spring (check with the Ranger District on water availability dates). Bring sleeping bags, pillows, matches, lantern, candles, bug repellent, flashlight with good batteries, garbage bags, axe, shovel, and water bucket (needed for outdoor campfires only), towels, soap, food (a convenience store is 15 minutes away), and toiletries including toilet paper.

HISTORY The cabin was constructed sometime in the 1930s. The Fremont Powerhouse Complex, of which Miner's Retreat is a part, offers visitors a glimpse into the area's rich mining history. In its heyday, the Fremont Powerhouse supplied electricity to nearby mines and towns. An electric company owned and utilized the Powerhouse and residential buildings until 1967. In 1968, the site was donated to the Forest Service. Since then, the buildings were occasionally used for employee housing and interpretive purposes. In 2001, the site was added to the recreation rental program.

AROUND YOU The cabin is located near the historic town of Granite, the North fork John Day Wilderness Area and the Elkhorn and Blue Mountain Scenic Byways. There are numerous recreational opportunities in this area of the Blue Mountains: sightseeing, horseback riding, and hiking. Olive Lake, located 8 miles west of the cabin, is a fine spot for fishing, camping, boating, and hiking.

FOR MORE INFORMATION
North Fork John Day Ranger District
P.O. Box 158
Ukiah, Oregon 97880
(541) 427-3231
http://www.fs.fed.us/r6/uma/recreation/cabins/nfcabins.shtml

> *"Come on in. The earth, like the sun, like the air,*
> *belongs to everyone—and to no one."*
>
> Edward Abbey

47 Congo Gulch Cabin

YOUR BEARINGS

59 miles southeast of Ukiah, Oregon
40 miles west of Baker City, Oregon
5 miles west of Granite, Oregon

AVAILABILITY Year-round, however the cabin may be closed occasionally for administrative needs and maintenance. Access to motor vehicles is open during the late spring, summer, and early fall months. In winter, access is by over-snow transportation (skis, snowshoes or snowmobiles). During these months, vehicle parking is off-site. Check with the Ranger District for current weather and road conditions prior to your arrival.

CAPACITY A maximum of six adults, with sleeping accommodations for four. Dogs are welcome at the cabin provided the owner picks up after them. Be aware that the structure has D-Con (rodent poison) placed within its perimeters. If you allow pets to wander freely, please keep them from disturbing wildlife and vegetation.

Congo Gulch Cabin

DESCRIPTION The cabin is a two-story, wood frame structure, with three bedrooms, a bathroom, kitchen, and living room area. The cabin has wood siding, tin roofing, and a cement foundation. A concrete walkway leads to the front porch steps and an enclosed rear entry is located off the kitchen for back-door access.

COST $50 per night.

RESERVATIONS Call the toll-free National Recreation Reservation Service (1-877-444-6777) or make your reservations online at www.ReserveUSA.com. Reservations are limited to 14 consecutive nights during a 30-day period, from noon to noon.

HOW TO GET THERE From Ukiah, proceed on Camas Street in a southeast direction (it becomes County Road 1475 at the city limits) for approximately 6 miles. Here, at the National Forest boundary it becomes Forest Service Road 52. Continue on Forest Road 52 for 40 miles to the North Fork John Day Campground. At this location, Forest Service Road 52 becomes Forest Service Road 73. Continue on Road 73 for 8 miles to the junction of Forest Service Road 73 and forest Service Road 10. The town of Granite is on the left side of the road. Travel west on Forest Road 10 for 5 miles to the Fremont Powerhouse Complex. The cabin is the only residence on the right side of the Powerhouse Complex entrance area.

ELEVATION 4939 feet

WHAT IS PROVIDED During the summer and fall months, potable water is available on site, as well as the luxury of indoor plumbing. During the winter and early spring months, the plumbing is shut down. Water will need to be carried in during this time. An outhouse is on site.

On a year-round basis the cabin is equipped with electric heat, light, refrigerator, stove/oven, beds, living room furniture, kitchen table, chairs, some kitchen gear (skillets, coffee pot, glasses, cups, dishes, silverware), and storage areas. Cleaning supplies are also provided. Pack out your trash, please.

WHAT TO BRING Water during late fall, winter, and early spring (check with the Ranger District on water availability dates). Bring sleeping bags, pillows, matches, lantern, candles, bug repellent, flashlight with good batteries, garbage bags, axe, shovel, and water bucket (needed for outdoor campfires only), towels, soap, food (a convenience store is 15 minutes away), and toiletries including toilet paper.

HISTORY The cabin was constructed sometime in the 1930s. The Fremont Powerhouse Complex, of which Congo Gulch Cabin is a part, offers visitors a glimpse into the area's rich mining history. In its heyday, the Fremont Powerhouse supplied electricity to nearby mines and towns. An electric company owned and utilized the Powerhouse and residential buildings until 1967. In 1968, the site was donated to the Forest

Service. Since then, the buildings were occasionally used for employee housing and interpretive purposes. In 2001, the site was added to the recreation rental program.

AROUND YOU The cabin is located near the historic town of Granite, the North fork John Day Wilderness Area and the Elkhorn and Blue Mountain Scenic Byways. There are numerous recreational opportunities in this area of the Blue Mountains: sightseeing, horseback riding, and hiking. Olive Lake, located 8 miles west of the cabin, is a fine spot for fishing, camping, boating, and hiking.

FOR MORE INFORMATION
North Fork John Day Ranger District
P.O. Box 158
Ukiah, Oregon 97880
(541) 427-3231
http://www.fs.fed.us/r6/uma/recreation/cabins/nfcabins.shtml

"Art is a harmony parallel with nature."

Paul Cézanne

48 Hilltop Hideaway

YOUR BEARINGS
59 miles southeast of Ukiah, Oregon
40 miles west of Baker City, Oregon
5 miles west of Granite, Oregon

AVAILABILITY Year-round, however the cabin may be closed occasionally for administrative needs and maintenance. Access to motor vehicles is open during the late spring, summer, and early fall months. In winter, access is by over-snow transportation (skis, snowshoes or snowmobiles). During these months, vehicle parking is off-site. Check with the Ranger District for current weather and road conditions prior to your arrival.

CAPACITY 2 people maximum. Dogs are welcome at the cabin provided the owner picks up after them. Be aware that the structure has D-Con (rodent poison) placed within its perimeters. If you allow pets to wander freely, please keep them from disturbing wildlife and vegetation.

DESCRIPTION This small cabin consists of one bedroom, a bathroom, kitchen, and living room area. It has wood siding, a tin roof and a cement foundation. The front porch (with steps) is accessed via a sloped lawn area in front of the residence. A second entry is provided by a back door off the kitchen. A gravel access road is located behind the cabin.

Two other cabins, Congo Gulch Cabin and Miner's Retreat, are also available for rent here at the Fremont Powerhouse Complex.

COST $30 per night.

RESERVATIONS Call the toll-free National Recreation Reservation Service (1-877-444-6777) or make your reservations online at www.ReserveUSA.com. Reservations are limited to 14 consecutive nights during a 30-day period, from noon to noon.

HOW TO GET THERE From Ukiah, proceed on Camas Street in a southeast direction (it becomes County Road 1475 at the city limits) for approximately 6 miles. Here, at the National Forest boundary it becomes Forest Service Road 52. Continue on Forest Road 52 for 40 miles to the North Fork John Day Campground. At this location, Forest Service Road 52 becomes Forest Service Road 73. Continue on Road 73 for 8 miles to the junction of Forest Service Road 73 and forest Service Road 10. The town of Granite is on the left side of the road. Travel west on Forest Road 10 for 5 miles to the Fremont Powerhouse Complex. The cabin is the uppermost residence in the complex.

ELEVATION 4939 feet

WHAT IS PROVIDED On a year-round basis, the cabin is equipped with oil heating, electricity, lighting, refrigerator, stove/oven, beds, living room furniture, kitchen table, chairs, some kitchen tools (skillets, coffee pot, glasses, cups, dishes, silverware), and storage areas. Cleaning supplies are provided. During the summer months, potable water is on site, as well as the luxury of indoor plumbing. During all other seasons, neither water nor indoor plumbing is available. Water for drinking, cooking,

Hilltop Hideaway

and washing will need to be carried in. There is an outhouse located on site.

WHAT TO BRING Water during late fall, winter and early spring (check with the Ranger District on water availability dates). Bring sleeping bags, pillows, matches, lantern, candles, bug repellent, flashlight with good batteries, garbage bags, axe, shovel and water bucket (needed for outdoor campfires only), towels, soap, food (a convenience store is 15 minutes away), and toiletries including toilet paper.

HISTORY The cabin was constructed sometime in the 1930s. The Fremont Powerhouse Complex, of which Congo Gulch Cabin is a part, offers visitors a glimpse into the area's rich mining history. In its heyday, the Fremont Powerhouse supplied electricity to nearby mines and towns. An electric company owned and utilized the Powerhouse and residential buildings until 1967. In 1968, the site was donated to the Forest Service. Since then, the buildings were occasionally used for employee housing and interpretive purposes. In 2001, the site was added to the recreation rental program.

AROUND YOU The cabin is located near the historic town of Granite, the North fork John Day Wilderness Area, and the Elkhorn and Blue Mountain scenic byways. There are numerous recreational opportunities in this area of the Blue Mountains: sightseeing, horseback riding, and hiking. Olive Lake, located 8 miles west of the cabin, is a fine spot for fishing, camping, boating, and hiking.

FOR MORE INFORMATION
North Fork John Day Ranger District
P.O. Box 158
Ukiah, Oregon 97880
(541) 427-3231
http://www.fs.fed.us/r6/uma/recreation/cabins/nfcabins.shtml

The Road Not Taken

Two roads diverged in a yellow wood,
And sorry I could not travel both
And be one traveler, long I stood
And looked down one as far as I could
To where it bent in the undergrowth;

Then took the other, as just as fair
And having perhaps the better claim,
Because it was grassy and wanted wear;
Though as for that, the passing there
Had worn them really about the same,

And both that morning equally lay
In leaves no step had trodden black
Oh, I kept the first for another day!
Yet knowing how way leads on to way,
I doubted if I should ever come back.

I shall be telling this with a sigh
Somewhere ages and ages hence:
Two roads diverged in a wood, and I—
I took the one less traveled by,
And that has made all the difference.

Robert Frost

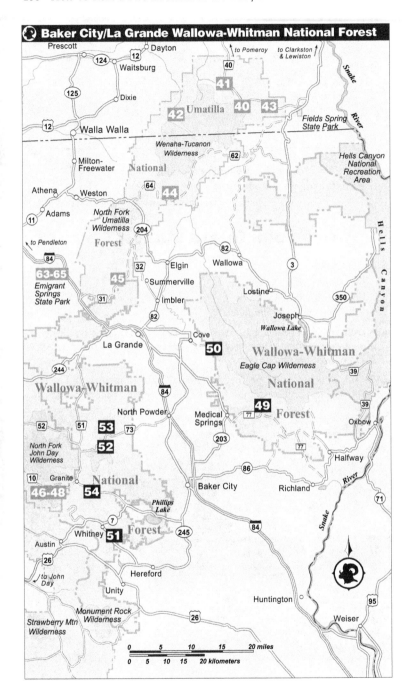

Baker City/La Grande Wallowa-Whitman National Forest

Wallowa-Whitman National Forest

"And to glance with an eye or show a bean in its pod confounds the learning of all times..."

Walt Whitman, "Song of Myself"

49 Two Color Guard Station

YOUR BEARINGS

45 miles northeast of Baker City
69 miles southeast of La Grande
105 miles southeast of Pendleton

AVAILABILITY Year-round. Experience Two Color Guard Station during the alpine winter when it is accessible only by snowmobile via a network of backcountry groomed trails.

CAPACITY As many as 12 people, though half that number would be more comfortable. Ideal for families. Pets okay if kept outside and leashed.

Two Color Guard Station

DESCRIPTION This is a fully accessible, barrier-free getaway. Water in the cabin is potable in summer, non-potable in winter. Indoor plumbing and a shower services summer guests only.

COST From $80 for one to four people to $160 for 12 people during the summer season (May 1 to September 30). From $60 for one to four people to $140 for 12 people during the winter season (October 1 to April 30).

RESERVATIONS The cabin is rented from 1:00 P.M. on your first day until noon on your last day. Call the toll-free National Recreation Reservation Service (1-877-444-6777) or make your reservations online at www.ReserveUSA.com.

HOW TO GET THERE For much of the winter the final 16 miles into the cabin are navigable only by snowmobile. The guard station is located at an elevation that gets sudden and heavy snowfall. Even with a small accumulation the access road can be dangerous. In winter, especially, keep posted on the weather reports and contact the Ranger Station for current conditions and advisories just prior to your trip.

There are no signs along the way for Two Color Guard Station. From Baker City, Oregon, travel six miles north on Interstate 84. Exit east at the sign for MEDICAL SPRINGS onto Highway 203, and follow it for 20 miles to Medical Springs. There, turn right, following the sign for BOULDER PARK. This is Big Creek Road, which becomes Forest Road 67.

After 17 miles beyond Medical Springs—17 long, winding, contorted, washboarded, gravel miles with extraordinarily lovely views of surrounding mountain peaks still covered in snow, even in July—you will be glad to reach Forest Road 77. Turn left.

You are now beside roaring, foaming, exquisite Eagle Creek. After less than a mile, Forest Road 77 veers off to the left, but you continue straight on Forest Road 7755, also called Two Color Road. After 1.5 miles be on the lookout for Two Color Guard Station. It is on the right and easy to miss—-but well past the Two Color Campground.

ELEVATION 4825 feet

WHAT IS PROVIDED Two Color Guard Station is more than a cabin in the woods, it's a small lodge. At the Guard Station you will find most utensils for cooking and eating, a gas stove, comfortable furnishings, enough beds to sleep a dozen, and indoor plumbing during the summer. You'll find propane lights, heating and cooking stoves, refrigerator, and water heater. The Guard Station faces Eagle Creek, has a spacious yard for outdoor activities, and a corral large enough for several stock animals.

WHAT TO BRING Bring camping supplies as well as garbage bags (pack it in, pack it out), candles or a lantern for emergencies, first aid kit, sleeping bag/bedding, toiletries, washcloths and towels, dish soap, and bar soap.

HISTORY Built in 1959 as a backcountry residence for field crews working on the La Grande Ranger District.

AROUND YOU Tucked away in a secluded corner of Wallowa-Whitman National Forest in northeastern Oregon, the cabin is just a two-hour drive from civilization. It overlooks a riparian marsh along the banks of Eagle Creek, which is noted for its rainbow trout.

In early July, when we were here, especially in the late evening, what was even louder than the gurgling of Eagle Creek was the offensive laughter of mosquitoes with stingers sharp enough to penetrate a coat of medieval armor. Maybe we had been in the woods too long, but it seemed at the time they were laughing at our mosquito repellent.

The Guard Station is 2 miles from the Boulder Park Trailhead, where trails lead into the Eagle Cap Wilderness. Abundantly stocked rainbow trout swim in Eagle Creek, just 150 feet from the Guard Station's front door. During the winter months you will find miles of roads and trails for snowmobiling.

If steep and rugged hikes to mountain lakes interest you, Eagle Cap Wilderness, which has no less than 18 mountains over 9000 feet, is just two miles northeast at the end of Forest Road 7755. Here you will find Boulder Park Trail 1922, which connects to Trail 1921—for Culver Lake (5.2 miles), Bear Lake (3.8 miles), and Looking Glass Lake (6.2 miles); and Trail 1931 for Eagle Lake and other glorious destinations beyond.

FOR MORE INFORMATION
La Grande Ranger District
3502 Hwy. 30
La Grande, Oregon 97850
(541) 963-7186
http://www.fs.fed.us/r6/w-w/recreation/cabin/cabin-info.shtml

"Come forth into the light of things. Let nature be your teacher."

William Wordsworth

50 Moss Springs Guard Station

YOUR BEARINGS
26 miles east of La Grande, Oregon

AVAILABILITY Year-round.

CAPACITY Sleeps up to five people inside (and five more outside).

DESCRIPTION A quaint cabin in the woods complete with many of the comforts of home.

COST $60 for one to four persons, each additional person is $10 per night.

RESERVATIONS Call the toll-free National Recreation Reservation Service (1-877-444-6777) or make your reservations online at www.ReserveUSA.com.

HOW TO GET THERE From Island City take Highway 237 to Cove. In Cove turn South onto County Road 65 (at Church across from High School), follow County Road 65 then Forest Road 6220, approximately 8.2 miles from church. Turn left onto Forest Road 6220-380 to Moss Springs Guard Station.

ELEVATION 6000 feet

WHAT IS PROVIDED In the summer months, running water, cold only, is available. Year-round enjoy propane lights, heating, and cook stove. A refrigerator and cooking and eating utensils are also provided. An outhouse is nearby the cabin.

WHAT TO BRING Bring camping supplies as well as garbage bags (pack it in, pack it out), candles or a lantern for emergencies, first aid kit, sleeping bag/bedding, toiletries, washcloths and towels, dish soap, and bar soap.

HISTORY Historic Moss Springs Guard station, eligible for the Register of Historic Places, was built as a backcountry ranger station in the 1920s. For decades, Moss Springs Guard Station fell into disrepair until now. Today, Moss Springs is as good as new.

AROUND YOU Enjoy extensive trail opportunities just up the road at Moss Springs Trailhead and the Breshears OHV Trails. Recreational activities

Moss Springs Guard Station

available in the vicinity include: hiking, mountain biking, horse trails, Nordic ski trails, and snowmobile trails.

FOR MORE INFORMATION
La Grande Ranger District
3502 Hwy. 30
La Grande, Oregon 97850
(541) 963-7186
http://www.fs.fed.us/r6/w-w/recreation/cabin/cabin-info.shtml

---

"It is a great art to saunter."

Henry David Thoreau, *Journal*, April 26, 1841

51 Antlers Guard Station

YOUR BEARINGS
21 miles northwest of Unity
35 miles northeast of Prairie City
40 miles west of Baker City
80 miles southwest of La Grande
130 miles south of Pendleton

AVAILABILITY Year-round.

CAPACITY Enough beds to sleep up to six people. This cabin is ideal for families. Pets okay if kept outdoors and leashed.

DESCRIPTION A very pleasant, rustic, furnished, and well-maintained two-room cabin—with a yard enclosed by a charming split rail fence.

COST $40 per night.

RESERVATIONS You can make reservations for up to seven consecutive nights, from noon on your arrival day and 10:00 A.M. on your departure day. Call the toll-free National Recreation Reservation Service (1-877-444-6777) or make your reservations online at www.ReserveUSA.com.

HOW TO GET THERE From Prairie City, Oregon, travel northeast on Highway 26 for 16 miles; turn left on Highway 7 and follow it north and northeast for 17 miles to County Road 529. Turn right on Road 529. This gravel road goes through the abandoned town of Whitney. After 2.5 miles on Road 529 you will see Antlers Guard Station on the left, tucked away under a steep hillside.

From Baker City, Oregon, travel south and then west on Highway 7 (part of the Elkhorn Scenic Byway), past 2400-acre Phillips Reservoir. Remain on Highway 7 until you reach County Road 529, about 38 miles. Turn left (south) onto Road 529, and travel through the abandoned Whitney town site. Antlers Guard Station is about 2.5 miles south on this gravel road, on the left.

From Unity, Oregon, travel north on Highway 26 approximately two miles, to Highway 245. Turn right. Continue on Highway 245 for approximately six miles to County Road 535. Turn left and continue northwest on Road 535—which becomes Road 529—and meanders alongside the North Fork of the Burnt River on its way to Antlers Guard Station, which is on the right side of the road.

During the winter months, Roads 529 and 535 are plowed intermittently. Contact the Ranger District in Unity for current road conditions. Snow may get deep in the driveway and high clearance vehicles, chains, or shovels are recommended.

ELEVATION 4107 feet

WHAT IS PROVIDED Propane lights, propane stove and oven, and a woodstove. Draw fresh potable water from the hand pump in the front yard and walk a short path to an outhouse, picnic table, and fire ring.

WHAT TO BRING Bring camping supplies as well as garbage bags (pack it in, pack it out), candles or a lantern for emergencies, first aid kit, sleeping bag/bedding, toiletries, washcloths and towels, dish soap, and bar soap.

HISTORY Built by the Civilian Conservation Corps in the 1930s and used as the field headquarters for fire patrols.

Antlers Guard Station

AROUND YOU It is legal to pan for gold in this section of the Burnt River, which flows through the backyard. Although we found no holes in the immediate vicinity big enough to actually swim in, there were several spots in the river suitable for wading.

Located along the North Fork Burnt River, the Guard Station is in a peaceful and remote setting. It is two miles from the historic town site of Whitney. Whitney once had a population of 150, but the entire town closed down when the trains stopped running through this area.

FOR MORE INFORMATION
Unity Ranger District
P.O. Box 39
Unity, Oregon 97884
(541) 446-3351
http://www.fs.fed.us/r6/w-w/recreation/cabin/cabin-info.shtml

"Time is but a stream I go a-fishing in."

Henry David Thoreau

52 Peavy Cabin

YOUR BEARINGS
47 miles northwest of Baker City
60 miles southwest of La Grande
90 miles south of Pendleton

AVAILABILITY January–March and July–December.

CAPACITY Six people. Ideal for families. Pets are welcome if they remain outdoors, are kept on a leash, and owners clean up after them.

DESCRIPTION The one-room cabin contains a fireplace, woodstove, gas range, refrigerator, lights, sink, large table, and benches, and enough beds to sleep four people. There is no water, no electricity, and no indoor bathroom. An outside vault toilet is located near the cabin. Some cooking and food serving utensils are provided. The grounds are partially fenced and include a horse corral and wood sheds.

COST $40 per night for up to six people. Larger parties will be considered at an additional $5 per person.

RESERVATIONS Available for up to 10 consecutive days from 2:00 P.M. on your day of arrival to noon on your day of departure. Call the toll-free National Recreation Reservation Service (1-877-444-6777) or make your reservations online at www.ReserveUSA.com.

HOW TO GET THERE From Baker City, Oregon, take Highway 30 north to Haines. Haines was known in the good old days as the town with "whiskey in the water and gold in the street." From Haines, turn west onto County Road 1146 and follow the elkhorn drive scenic byway signs to Anthony Lakes, 34.4 miles. Continue for another 12.5 miles past the ski resort, past the Elkhorn Summit, and down to the North Fork John Day River and Forest Road 380, which is on the left. By now you will have traveled about 47 miles from Baker City. At the junction of Forest Road 380 there is a sign: peavy cabin 3, cunningham cove 3, trail 1643.

The road, paved all the way, passes through some of the grandest scenery to be found anywhere. Elkhorn Summit, at 7392 feet, is the highest ground to be reached by paved road in all of Oregon. The snow-covered peaks of the Elkhorn seem close enough to reach out and touch.

When you turn left onto Forest Road 380 you will see a sign that reads rough road ahead. not recommended for passenger cars. Pay heed to this sign—park your car and walk. We made it all the way driving a 1971 Datsun pick-up, but only by getting out every now and then, especially during the last mile, to measure with a stick the depth of the water in the pools that completely hid the road—if one can call it that. Anyway, Thoreau would definitely want you to walk the rest of the way. The road follows the wonderful North Fork John Day River all the way to the cabin.

Peavy Cabin

In winter, Forest Road 73 is not plowed beyond the Anthony Lakes Ski Area. Contact Baker Ranger District for current weather and road conditions

In spring when the snow is melting, and during rainy weather any time of year, road conditions can be hazardous due to washouts and possibly high water on the road. Please ask for current road conditions prior to driving the road. In winter, access is by snowmobile on the groomed route from Granite or the Anthony Lakes Ski Area. The last 3 miles on Forest Road 380 are not groomed.

ELEVATION 5800 feet

WHAT IS PROVIDED Enjoy here a fireplace; woodstove; gas range, refrigerator, lights, sink, large table and benches, and enough beds to sleep four people. There is no water, no electricity, and no indoor bathroom. An outside vault toilet is located near the cabin. Some cooking and food serving utensils are provided.

WHAT TO BRING Enough drinking water for the length of your stay. Bring camping gear, matches, candle or lantern, flashlights, trash bags, first aid kit, towels, soap, toiletries, and food.

SETTING If we were to be given the frightening task of finding a cabin to rent for no less an expert than Henry David Thoreau, we would, we are confident, after consulting his friend Emerson, choose Peavy Cabin. No other cabin in this book comes as close to Thoreau's most exacting criteria for a place to live.

One of the many reasons Peavy Cabin is so close to Thoreau's ideal is that it is situated on the edge of a wilderness, the North Fork John Day; another reason is that it is on the bank of a river, the North Fork of the John Day; and yet another is that a tiny stream flows by the house—through the front yard in fact. And, being the sturdy soul Thoreau undoubtedly was, there is Lost Lake, to which he could hike—or saunter, as he would prefer.

And, perhaps, even more important to Thoreau than any of these, would be that the cabin's location allows for solitude and seclusion. This, too, Peavy does, in great and generous measure, though this makes it quite difficult to get to.

It is set in a large and level meadow; on the day we were there in mid-July, there was a lovely stream of the clearest water flowing by. The cabin itself is exquisite in almost every detail, with log and stone blending beautifully together. The floors are of polished wood, the ceiling beams are unhewn, the fireplace is of solid stone, the woodstove is waist-high, the chairs and table seem especially made and designed for this cabin, and even the pots and pans hanging on the wall seem to belong to another, sturdier era.

HISTORY Built in 1934 by Dr. George Wilcox Peavy, Dean of the School of Forestry at Oregon Agricultural College (later Oregon State University), who used it as an office for his field laboratory work. Its integrity and charm have survived several restoration projects, and it is now recorded in the Heritage Resource Inventory as an historic site.

AROUND YOU Secluded on the edge of wilderness, Peavy Cabin stands between a dense alpine forest and an open meadow.

Adjacent to the cabin, the Peavy Trailhead provides access to the North Fork John Day Wilderness via the Peavy Trail (1640) and the Cunningham Cove Trail (1643). Both trails connect with the Elkhorn Crest National Recreation Trail (1611). Sights of a recent forest fire are visible from the cabin and along the trails.

FOR MORE INFORMATION
Baker Ranger District
3165 10th Street
Baker City, Oregon 97814
(541) 523-4476
http://www.fs.fed.us/r6/w-w/recreation/cabin/peavy.shtml

"Take a course in good water and air; and in the eternal youth of Nature you may renew your own. Go quietly, alone; no harm will befall you."

John Muir

53 Anthony Lakes Guard Station

YOUR BEARINGS
35 miles northwest of Baker City, Oregon

AVAILABILITY Anthony Lakes Guard Station is available from May 1 to October 31.

CAPACITY Sleep up to eight people. Pets are welcome if they remain outdoors, are kept on a leash and owners clean up after them.

DESCRIPTION The cabin is a 1930s-era log dwelling with three bedrooms, located on the northern shore of Anthony Lake. It provides a spectacular view of the lake and surrounding glacial peaks.

COST $80 for one to four persons in the summer season (May 1–Oct. 31); each additional person is $10 per night.

RESERVATIONS Call the toll-free National Recreation Reservation Service (1-877-444-6777) or make your reservations online at www.ReserveUSA.com.

HOW TO GET THERE From Baker City, take highway 30 to Haines, turn west on County Road 1146, follow the Elkhorn Drive Scenic Byway signs to Anthony Lakes, turn left at the campground entrance. Anthony Lakes Guard station is located adjacent to the campground.

ELEVATION 7100 feet

WHAT IS PROVIDED Running water, electric lights, stove, refrigerator, and propane stove for heating and cooking. Eating utensils and place settings are provided. This is a comfortable cabin, complete with all the amenities of home in an alpine setting.

WHAT TO BRING Bring camping gear, matches, candle or lantern, flashlights, trash bags, first aid kit, towels, soap, toiletries, and food.

HISTORY The Civilian Conservation Corps built Anthony Lakes Guard Station, eligible for the National Register of Historic Places, as a backcountry ranger station in the 1930s. The purpose of the guard station was to provide information to Forest visitors and to provide fire watch.

AROUND YOU Hiking trail opportunities are nearby within the Elkhorn Mountains. In the heart of the Elkhorns, you'll have hundreds of miles of trails to access, or grab your fishing pole and go fishing in Anthony Lake just out the back door.

FOR MORE INFORMATION
Baker Ranger District
3165 10th Street
Baker City, Oregon 97814
(541) 523-4476
http://www.fs.fed.us/r6/
w-w/recreation/cabin/
cabin-info.shtml

Anthony Lakes Guard Station

*"Shall I not have intelligence with the earth?
Am I not partly leaves and vegetable mould myself?"*

Henry David Thoreau

54 Boundary Guard Station

YOUR BEARINGS Boundary Guard Station is 3 miles southeast from the historic town of Granite, along the Elkhorn Scenic Byway. Boundary Guard Station is available year round, 42 miles west of Baker City off of the paved scenic byway.

AVAILABILITY Year-round.

CAPACITY Sleeps up to eight people. Pets are welcome if they remain outdoors, are kept on a leash and owners clean up after them.

DESCRIPTION An historic two-story rustic cabin adjacent to Boundary Creek.

COST From June 1 to September 30 (summer season) is $60 per night for one to four people; plus $10 per night for each additional person. From October 1 to May 31 (winter season) is $40 per night for one to four people; plus $10 per night for each additional person.

RESERVATIONS Available for a maximum stay of 10 consecutive days, the cabin is reserved from 2:00 P.M. on your arrival day to noon on your

Boundary Guard Station

departure day. Call the toll-free National Recreation Reservation Service (1-877-444-6777) or make your reservations online at www.ReserveUSA.com.

HOW TO GET THERE From Baker City, travel State Highway 7 to the Sumpter turnoff. Follow Highway 410 to the town of Sumpter. Continue through Sumpter and follow the Elkhorn Drive Scenic Byway past Blue Springs Summit to Boundary Guard Station. The area receives several feet of snow in the winter months. Although the county road to the cabin is plowed, the renter must park adjacent to the highway and possibly break trail through the snow 100 feet or so to the cabin.

ELEVATION 4700 feet

WHAT IS PROVIDED The rustic cabin is heated with a propane fireplace. The kitchen has an electric stove and refrigerator. Also, on the ground floor are a living room with a futon couch and one bedroom. Upstairs are two large bedrooms. For summer use only, there is a bathroom with sink, flush toilet, and shower. Water is available only during the summer and is shut off in winter. An outhouse is provided for winter use. Picnic tables are located on the grounds. Outside is enough camping area to accommodate at least eight more guests.

WHAT TO BRING In winter, bring enough water for all your drinking, cooking, and washing needs for the length of your stay. Also bring sleeping bag, matches, candles, lantern, flashlight, trash bags, first aid kit, towels, soap, toiletries, and food.

HISTORY Boundary Guard Station was built sometime prior to 1926, adjacent to Boundary Creek on the Baker Ranger District. It served as an administrative office and fire crew quarters. It is eligible for the National Register of Historic Places.

AROUND YOU In the heart of snow country, you'll have hundreds of miles of groomed trails to access, or strap on your skis or snowshoes and enjoy the snow right out the back door. Numerous hiking trails within the Elkhorn Mountains and North Fork John Day Wilderness are nearby. Remote mountain lakes and the North Fork John Day River provide excellent fishing.

FOR MORE INFORMATION
Baker Ranger District
3165 10th Street
Baker City, Oregon 97814
(541) 523-4476
http://www.fs.fed.us/r6/w-w/recreation/cabin/cabin-info.shtml

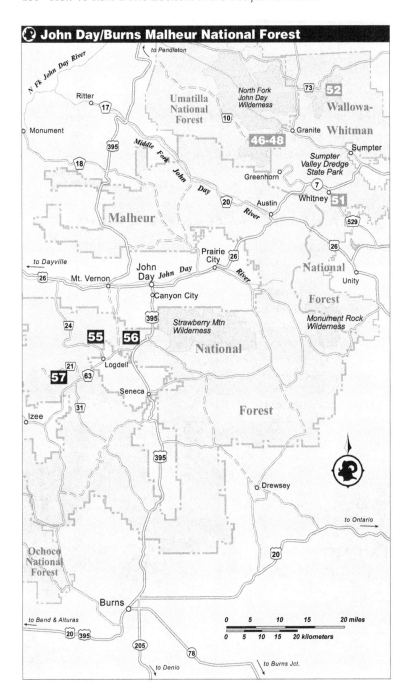

John Day/Burns Malheur National Forest

N Fk John Day River

to Pendleton

Ritter
17

Monument

18
395

Middle Fork John Day

Umatilla
National
Forest
10

North Fork
John Day
Wilderness

73   52

Wallowa-

Granite   Whitman

46-48

Sumpter
Valley Dredge
State Park

Sumpter

Greenhorn

20

Austin

7

Whitney   51

529

Malheur

26

to Dayville

26   Mt. Vernon

John
Day   John Day

Prairie
City   26

John Day River

26

National

Unity

Forest

Monument Rock
Wilderness

Canyon City

24

55   56

395

Strawberry Mtn
Wilderness

National

21
57   63

Logdell

Seneca

31

Izee

Forest

395

Drewsey

to Ontario

Ochoco
National
Forest

Burns

to Bend & Alturas

20   395

205

78

to Denio

to Burns Jct.

0   5   10   15   20 miles
0   5   10   15   20 kilometers

Malheur National Forest

*"I believe in the forest, and in the meadow,
and in the night in which the corn grows."*

Henry David Thoreau,
"A Plea for Captain John Brown," 1859

55 Murderer's Creek Work Center

YOUR BEARINGS

Approximately 32 miles southwest of the town of John Day
75 miles northwest of Burns
165 miles south of Pendleton
185 miles east of Bend

AVAILABILITY Approximately mid-May to mid-November; only when
access by passenger vehicle can safely be achieved. No rentals are available during the winter season.

CAPACITY A maximum of four people. This rental is ideal for families. Pets
are welcome if they stay outdoors, are kept on a leash, and owners
clean up after them.

Murderer's Creek Work Center

DESCRIPTION This facility consists of two cabins. The main cabin or cookhouse is equipped with kitchen, bathroom with shower, wood heat, propane cook stove, and propane refrigerator. The other cabin or bunkhouse has two bedrooms, propane heaters, and four twin beds.

COST $40 per night.

RESERVATIONS May be rented for a maximum of 14 consecutive nights. Call the toll-free National Recreation Reservation Service (1-877-444-6777) or make your reservations online at www.ReserveUSA.com.

HOW TO GET THERE There are two ways to access this facility. The Izee Highway, County Road 63, is 17 miles south of the town of John Day, off Highway 395, or about 55 miles north of Burns. Take the Izee Highway west off Highway 395 for six miles to Forest Road 21. Turn right onto Forest Road 21, and continue for 12 miles, following the signs for MURDERER'S CREEK. It is paved all the way except for the final two miles. The guard station is on the left.

Another access is from John Day. Travel west on Highway 26 approximately 18 miles. Turn left onto Forest Service Road 21. Travel Forest Service Road 21 approximately 14 miles to the work center.

ELEVATION 5000 feet

WHAT IS PROVIDED Woodstove, propane cook stove, propane light, table and chairs, four single beds with mattresses, a couch, and a chest of drawers.

There are two structures here, the cabin, and the sleeping quarters. They are rented simultaneously. The cabin, built in 1906, is thought to be the oldest Ranger Station in the Pacific Northwest—your sausages will be sauteed in history.

There is a good kitchen with fridge, sinks, closets, counter-tops, and faucets. Do not drink the water, though, or you may be history too. There is a bathroom with shower in the cabin.

The sleeping quarters were built more than 75 year after the cabin, so they are purely functional. There are two bedrooms with large closets—large by cabin standards anyway.

There is no water, no electricity, and no indoor restroom. There is an outdoor vault toilet located in close proximity of the house.

WHAT TO BRING Food and beverages, the facility key (provided by the Forest Service), flashlight with extra batteries, first aid equipment, matches and lighter, sleeping bags, and bedding. Bring drinking water, camera and film, garbage bags—the Forest has a pack-it-in–pack-it-out policy—firewood for outdoor fires, dish towels/soap and toiletries/tissue.

HISTORY The main cabin, constructed in 1906, still serves its original purpose as a summer home for fire-crews. As to the name "Murderer's Creek," perhaps some remorseful murderer sought forgiveness here by its green banks. Local lore has it that early settlers here were killed by Native Americans.

AROUND YOU Murderer's Creek is murmuring in your backyard on its way west to meet the South Fork John Day River. The Aldrich Mountain/Murderer's Creek Wildlife Area, an undesignated wilderness, is nearby. Riley Creek Trailhead (216A) is to the northeast, at the end of Forest Road 2190 which is off Forest Road 21, a few miles east of the cabin.

Fields Peak Trailhead (212) is to the north at the end of Spur Road 125, which is also off Forest Road 21 a few miles north of the cabin.

Trail 212 joins Trail 216, which goes around McClellan Mountain rising to 7042 feet. From Fields Peak to Riley Creek trailheads is 10.5 miles.

Bighorn sheep were hunted to extinction in the nearby Aldrich Mountain/Murderer's Creek Wildlife Area. In 1978 they were reintroduced: it is thought that there are as many as 60 of these animals there today. There are also pronghorn antelope, elk, mule deer, mountain lions, and, usually, not many people.

This is wild country. If you use any of these trails, take water, a topographic map, and compass. Herds of wild horses are often seen around the cabin. We waited in vain for them to come and drag us away.

FOR MORE INFORMATION
Blue Mountain Ranger District
P.O. Box 909
431 Patterson Bridge Rd.
John Day, OR 97845
(541) 575-3000
http://www.fs.fed.us/r6/malheur/
http://www.fs.fed.us/r6/w-w/recreation/cabin/cabin-info.shtml

*"To me every hour of the light and dark is a miracle,
every cubic inch of space is a miracle."*

Walt Whitman, "Miracles"

56 Fall Mountain Lookout

YOUR BEARINGS
Approximately 14 miles southwest of John Day
70 miles north of Burns
150 miles south of Pendleton
170 miles west of Bend

AVAILABILITY Spring and summer seasons. Not available in winter.

CAPACITY Two people maximum. Pets are welcome if they stay outdoors, are kept on a leash, and owners clean up after them.

DESCRIPTION This facility is a 14 x 14 foot cabin atop a 25-foot tower. This facility is currently the only electric fire lookout available, with an electric cook stove, electric refrigerator, electric heater, and electric lights.

COST $40 per night.

RESERVATIONS Call the toll-free National Recreation Reservation Service (1-877-444-6777) or make your reservations online at www.ReserveUSA.com.

HOW TO GET THERE From the town of John Day travel south for about 15 miles on Highway 395 to Starr Campground. Turn right here onto Forest Road 4920 where you will then see the sign: FALL MOUNTAIN LOOKOUT 4. Travel northwest 3.5 miles to the very steep and unmaintained Forest Road 607 and turn left. The lookout is one mile ahead on this rough and steep road. There is parking for a couple of cars.

Fall Mountain Lookout

There is an alternative route off Highway 395. A few miles north of Starr Campground and just south of the Vance Creek rest area, turn right onto Forest Road 3920 and continue to Forest Road 607.

ELEVATION 5949 feet

WHAT IS PROVIDED This lookout is the only one in this rental program with electricity—the fridge, stove, heater and lights are all electric. There are chairs and a table, double bed, closets, fire extinguisher, shovel, maps for the area, and a vault toilet.

There is a futon for a bed that sleeps two comfortably. There is no water and no indoor restroom. A vault toilet is located in close proximity of the lookout.

WHAT TO BRING Food and beverages, the facility key (provided by the Forest Service), flashlight with extra batteries, first aid equipment, matches and lighter, sleeping bags, and bedding. Bring drinking water, camera and film, garbage bags—the Forest has a pack-it-in–pack-it-out policy—firewood for outdoor fires, dish towels/soap, and toiletries/tissue.

THE SETTING This is a beautifully situated lookout tower, though the sense of remoteness and isolation does suffer rather badly from a microwave thingamabob that looks like the work of deranged Martians. Unfortunately, it is only about 50 yards away from the lookout. But it is an ill-wind that doesn't blow some good: without the microwave thingamabob the lookout would not have electricity.

HISTORY Built in 1933. Back then there were miles of telephone wire stretched all the way from the lookout, through the woods, to the firefighters at Bear Valley Work Center.

AROUND YOU The winter shutters have been removed, giving a full 360-degree view of the surrounding valleys and the south side of the Strawberry Mountains. Looking to the north you can see the town of Mt. Vernon and looking to the south you can see the town of Seneca. Visitors can enjoy great sunsets and sunrises. On clear nights, witness spectacular views of the stars. Should you be lucky enough you may even have the opportunity to experience a phenomenal light show provided by a summer lightning storm.

FOR MORE INFORMATION
Blue Mountain Ranger District
P.O. Box 909
431 Patterson Bridge Rd.
John Day, OR 97845
(541) 575-3000
http://www.fs.fed.us/r6/malheur/
http://www.fs.fed.us/r6/w-w/recreation/cabin/cabin-info.shtml

"I know of no more encouraging fact than the unquestionable ability of man to elevate his life by conscious endeavor."

Henry David Thoreau, *Walden*

57 Deer Creek Guard Station

YOUR BEARINGS

Approximately 31 miles southwest of John Day
75 miles northwest of Burns
165 miles south of Pendleton
185 miles east of Bend

AVAILABILITY Approximately May through mid-November, weather conditions permitting.

CAPACITY A maximum of four people. Ideal for families.

DESCRIPTION 20 x 14-foot, one-room cabin, with bathroom and shower. In the spring and summer enjoy wildflowers, wild horses, wildlife viewing, and splendid peace and quiet.

COST $40 per night.

RESERVATIONS Call the toll-free National Recreation Reservation Service (1-877-444-6777) or make your reservations online at www.ReserveUSA.com.

HOW TO GET THERE The Izee Highway, County Road 63, is 17 miles south of the town of John Day off Highway 395, or about 55 miles north of Burns, off Highway 395. From here take the Izee Highway west for 10 miles to Forest Road 24. Turn right, and follow Forest Road 24 north

Deer Creek Guard Station

and then southwest for another nine miles to Forest Road 514. Turn left. The guard station is on the right, less than a half mile down this road. You will find plenty of parking space.

In winter, Forest Road 24 may not be plowed, so skis and snowshoes may be necessary. Access under such conditions can be moderate to difficult depending on snow accumulation. Check with the Bear Valley Ranger District for current road and weather conditions.

ELEVATION 5100 feet

WHAT IS PROVIDED The inside of the cabin has lovely tongue-and-groove pine paneling, high ceilings, curtained windows, and vinyl flooring. It is furnished with one set of twin bunk beds, one futon, and one couch to sleep four comfortably. This facility has wood heat and is equipped with a propane cook stove, propane refrigerator, and propane lights. There is NO water, NO electricity, and NO indoor restroom. An outdoor vault toilet is located in close proximity to the house.

WHAT TO BRING Food and beverages, the facility key (provided by the Forest Service), flashlight with extra batteries, first aid equipment, matches and lighter, sleeping bags, and bedding. Bring drinking water, camera and film, garbage bags—the Forest Service has a pack-it-in–pack-it-out policy—firewood for outdoor fires, dish towels/soap, and toiletries/tissue.

SETTING This small cabin is beautifully situated in a huge meadow that contains a massive ponderosa pine, said to be one of the biggest in the Malheur National Forest. Deer Creek is at one end of the meadow, on its way west to join the South Fork John Day River, and Dead Injun Creek babbles by the fire ring and barbecue area, on its way to meet Deer Creek.

HISTORY In 1956 the Forest Service built the guard station here to house a fire guard.

AROUND YOU We noticed a surprising number of old-growth trees between the cabin and Flag Tail Lookout, which is a couple of miles east. This entire area is a maze of old logging roads. You will surely find a gold mine down one of them. The cabin is on the brink of Aldrich Mountain/Murderer's Creek Wildlife Area, where you may encounter bighorn sheep, pronghorn antelope, mule deer, elk, and mountain lions.

FOR MORE INFORMATION
Blue Mountain Ranger District
P.O. Box 909
431 Patterson Bridge Rd.
John Day, OR 97845
(541) 575-3000
http://www.fs.fed.us/r6/malheur/
http://www.fs.fed.us/r6/w-w/recreation/cabin/cabin-info.shtml

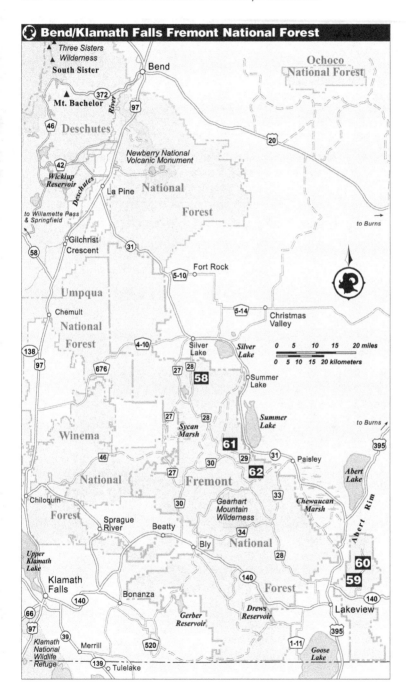

Bend/Klamath Falls Fremont National Forest

Three Sisters
Wilderness
South Sister
Bend
Ochoco
National Forest

Mt. Bachelor 372

97

46 Deschutes

Newberry National
Volcanic Monument

20

42

Wickiup
Reservoir

La Pine National

Forest

to Willamette Pass
& Springfield

to Burns

Gilchrist
Crescent

58 31

Fort Rock

5-10

Umpqua

Chemult

5-14

Christmas
Valley

National

Forest

138 4-10

Silver
Lake

Silver
Lake

0   5   10   15   20 miles

0 5 10 15 20 kilometers

97 676

27 28

58

Summer
Lake

27 28

Sycan
Marsh

Summer
Lake

to Burns

Winema

46

61

395

27

30

29 31

Paisley

Abert
Lake

National

30

62

Fremont

33

Chewaucan
Marsh

Chiloquin

Gearhart
Mountain
Wilderness

Forest

Sprague
River

Beatty

34

Bly National

28

Upper
Klamath
Lake

60

59

Klamath
Falls

140

Bonanza

140

Drews
Reservoir

140

Lakeview

66

97

Gerber
Reservoir

395

39

Klamath
National
Wildlife
Refuge

Merrill

520

1-11

Goose
Lake

139 Tulelake

Fremont National Forest

---

*"The ultimate finale was the parting of the clouds and a
vivid red sunset over Mt. Shasta."*

From the Lookout's Guestbook, 1994

58 Hager Mountain Lookout

YOUR BEARINGS

15 miles south of the town of Silver Lake
60 miles north of Bly
95 miles south of Bend
100 miles northeast of Klamath Falls

AVAILABILITY Rented from November through April 15.

CAPACITY Maximum of four, though two would be more comfortable.

DESCRIPTION 14 x 14-foot room with a jaunty hip roof and deck. In need
of some T.L.C., but with incomparable views.

COST $25 per night.

RESERVATIONS Call the toll-free National Recreation Reservation Service
(1-877-444-6777) or make your
reservations online at
www.ReserveUSA.com.

HOW TO GET THERE From the Silver
Lake Ranger District office, travel 0.5 mile east on Highway 31,
then turn right (south) onto
County Road 4-12, which
becomes Forest Road 28. Take
Road 28 for 11 miles, then turn
left onto Forest Road 036. This
gravel road is not signed until
you have turned onto it, and,
since it is at a bend in Forest
Road 28, it is very easily passed
by. As a guide, it is two miles
south of the TRAIL sign and about

Hagar Mountain Lookout

100 yards south of the SHARP CURVES 25 MPH sign. Turn left onto Road
036 and continue to Forest Road 497, about two miles ahead.

Here you will notice a sign: HAGER MOUNTAIN LOOKOUT 3—but don't
believe it, it is over four miles. Despite signs to the contrary, many cars,
at least in summer, should be able to negotiate this road for another 2.5
miles to the green gate. Here, though, all cars should park. The final
mile or so to the lookout from the locked green gate is extremely steep
with very sharp hair-pin bends, and should not be attempted in a vehicle that does not have four-wheel drive. Visitors on foot, snowshoes or
skis should be prepared for an arduous climb.

From Bly travel three miles west on Highway 140 to Ivory Pine
Road, also County Road 1257, which becomes Forest Road 036. To
continue on pavement, follow this road all the way to Forest Road 28—
about 30 miles ahead. Turn left onto Forest Road 28 and continue
north for about 24 miles, following the Silver Lake signs, to Forest
Road 036. This gravel road is not signed; it is on the right 3.5 miles
north of the sign: EAST BAY CAMPGROUND. Turn right onto 036 and continue for one mile to Forest Road 497, which is the access route (above)
to the lookout.

For hikers there are a few alternatives: one is from a trailhead which
is nine miles south of Highway 31 on Forest Road 28. It is signed and
has parking. The lookout is four miles away—but be forewarned, this
is a strenuous hike by most people's standards and may be too strenuous for some.

Another option is to turn left on unmaintained Forest Road 012,
which is off of Road 28 but is not signed—it is close to the trailhead
mentioned above. Continue on this road for about two miles, until it
ends. The lookout is now only two miles away, but, again, take heed,
that two miles has an elevation gain of 1600 feet. That may be about
1000 feet too much for some, but for others a welcome challenge.

Before approaching the lookout in winter, it is essential to check
with the Ranger District to determine your best method of travel. Snow
levels are apt to vary greatly from one year to the next, even one day to
the next. Skiing or snowshoeing from the parking area can take as long
as half a day depending on weather conditions and one's ability.

ELEVATION 7200 feet

WHAT IS PROVIDED Two cots, two beds, two fridges, a very small woodstove, and firewood; also a propane cook stove, two large pots for boil-
ing water, and a coffee pot, but no sink. An outhouse, horse tie-racks
and picnic table are close to the cabin but, according to some of the
comments in the guestbook, the outhouse is not nearly close enough.

Renting this lookout in winter is definitely for the adventurous, and
even those who consider themselves adventurous should also be fit and

enjoy coping with snow drifts, gale-force winds, and the possibility of nocturnal visits to an outhouse that is about 100 yards away.

WHAT TO BRING Drinking water is a must—none is provided. Snowmelt can be used for your washing needs, though safe drinking water from snow cannot be assured, so have the means to treat it. Bring extra food—severe weather conditions may delay your departure. And bring those binoculars, even if they do add a pound or two. You will have a fair amount of land and sky to survey.

SETTING Hager Mountain Lookout is one of a diminishing number of mountaintop sites still staffed by fire-guards throughout the summer and early fall. Although a trip to the summit is a very rewarding experience at any time of the year, the lookout may be rented only when the threat of wildfire has passed and the seasonal lookout personnel have returned home. So, dust off your skis; there are open slopes below the lookout, which in good snow years provide some spectacular telemark skiing opportunities.

HISTORY The original Hager Mountain Lookout was an L-4 ground-mounted type constructed in the 1920s from a kit. Its replacement was built in the 1960s. Better road access, reconnaissance flights, and satellite detection systems have decreased the number of fire lookouts in use on National Forest and State protected lands, but Hager Mountain Lookout continues to be staffed from June to October of each year.

AROUND YOU Though not available for rent during the summer or early fall, Hager Mountain Lookout is still a lovely destination. On a clear day you will be treated to a 360-degree panoramic view of the landscape from Mt. Shasta to Mt. Hood.

The trail from the lookout ends about 26 miles west at the summit of Yamsey Mountain, which is a Semi-Primitive Recreation Area, i.e., an undesignated wilderness, passing through Antler and Silver Creek Marsh Trailheads and Campgrounds. Thompson Reservoir is within five miles of Hager Mountain and has camping facilities on its east and west banks.

Near the lookout is a gravestone surrounded with flowers, placed here as a memorial to a former Hager Mountain lookout guard who died in a car crash.

FOR MORE INFORMATION
Silver Lake Ranger District
Highway 31
P.O. Box 129
Silver Lake, OR 97638
(541) 576-2107
http://www.fs.fed.us/r6/fremont/rogs/hagrlo.htm
http://www.fs.fed.us/r6/w-w/recreation/cabin/cabin-info.shtml

"I believe a leaf of grass is no less than the journey-work of the stars."

Walt Whitman, "Song of Myself"

59 Aspen Cabin

YOUR BEARINGS

25 miles northeast of Lakeview
120 miles east of Klamath Falls
200 miles southeast of Bend

AVAILABILITY The cabin is rented from June 1 through November 1. November through May it serves as a free public warming shelter centrally located to trails, fishing sites, and semi-primitive areas.

CAPACITY The cabin comfortably accommodates up to four people.

DESCRIPTION Lovely, historic log cabin in a delightful setting with fenced yard, outdoor picnic table, and fire pit.

COST $25 per night, from noon to noon. All rental profits from the cabin are used for its maintenance and preservation.

RESERVATIONS Call the toll-free National Recreation Reservation Service (1-877-444-6777) or make your reservations online at www.ReserveUSA.com.

Aspen Cabin

HOW TO GET THERE The route is paved all the way. From Lakeview travel five miles north on Highway 395 and turn right onto Highway 140. Go east on Highway 140 eight miles to North Warner Road (Forest Road 3615). Turn left and go north another eight miles, past aspen-fringed Bull Prairie and Mud Creek Campground. The cabin is on the right.

ELEVATION 6500 feet

WHAT IS PROVIDED Potable water is available at Mud Creek Campground. The cabin is furnished with a woodstove and dining table with chairs, and offers countertop space and an outdoor vault toilet.

WHAT TO BRING Food and beverages, the facility key (provided by the Forest Service), flashlight with extra batteries, first aid equipment, matches and lighter, sleeping bags and bedding. Bring drinking water, camera and film, garbage bags—the Forest has a pack-it-in–pack-it-out policy—firewood, dish towels/soap, and toiletries/tissue.

THE SETTING A log cabin enticingly situated among groves of aspen and stands of ponderosa pine and white fir. There is a heartwarming, foot-freezing little stream flowing just in front of the gate as deep as it is wide—about 12 inches.

In early July, when we were there, wildflowers and butterflies, almost indistinguishable from one another, were dancing on the banks of this stream and, indeed, all over the entire grounds. Unfortunately, in the evening, mosquitoes joined in and we too started dancing—all the way to our backpacks for repellent.

HISTORY This historic log cabin was built in 1930 and served as a Forest Service guard station through the late 1970s.

AROUND YOU Abert Rim, to the north, is 2000 feet high and more than 30 miles long, which makes it the highest exposed escarpment in North America. Thermal winds off Lake Abert make possible 20-mile hang-gliding flights along the length of the rim, and make Tague's Butte a well-known launching site.

To reach Tague's Butte continue north on Forest Road 3615 another 13 miles to the second entrance to the looped Forest Road 032. After 0.75 mile, take the spur road through the gate for about 0.5 mile. Tague's Butte juts out from Abert Rim and provides an expansive view of the valley, and Lake Abert.

On the 4th of July it is the site of the Annual Hang-Gliding Fly-In. On that weekend, in nearby Lakeview, there is not a vacant hotel room in town. Yet, on that same weekend, while people roamed the town searching in vain for a place to sleep, this delightful cabin, closer than any other accommodation to Tague's Butte, the actual hang-gliding launch site, was vacant.

To find the best view closest to the cabin, travel one mile west of the cabin and turn left onto Forest Road 019. Follow this to Drake Peak

Lookout which, in fact, is on Light Peak. You can reach Drake Peak itself via Spur Road 138 and hike one mile to the top.

There are numerous trails in the vicinity of the cabin, and trail information is available at the Ranger District. Some lead into the Drake-McDowell Semi-Primitive Non-Motorized Recreation Area. They are open to hikers, equestrians, and mountain-bikers. All have spacious trailheads for parking and trailer turnaround. All except the Swale trailhead have toilet facilities. The South Fork Crooked Creek Trail also has a horse feeder and tie racks. The Walker trail leads to the Crane Mountain National Recreation Trail.

FOR MORE INFORMATION
Lakeview Ranger District
HC 64, Box 60
Lakeview, Oregon 97630
(541) 947-3334
http://www.fs.fed.us/r6/fremont/rogs/aspencab.htm
http://www.fs.fed.us/r6/w-w/recreation/cabin/cabin-info.shtml

"Nobody sees a flower—really—it is so small it takes time—we haven't time—and to see takes time, like to have a friend takes time."

Georgia O'Keeffe

60 Drake Peak Lookout

YOUR BEARINGS
23 miles northeast of Lakeview, Oregon

AVAILABILITY The lookout should be available for rent from July 1 through October 15. In mild winters it may be available in late June. Reservations are on a first-come, first-served basis.

CAPACITY The lookout can accommodate up to four people but two would be more comfortable.

DESCRIPTION The lookout is an "L-4 Aladdin ground house cabin" that is 14 x 14 feet.

COST $25 per night with monies used directly for the maintenance of the lookout. The fee is charged per group per night.

RESERVATIONS Call the toll-free National Recreation Reservation Service (1-877-444-6777) or make your reservations online at www.ReserveUSA.com.

HOW TO GET THERE From Lakeview Ranger District Office go 2.5 miles north on Highway 395, and turn right on Highway 140. Take Highway 140 east for 8 miles. Here, turn left on Forest Road 3615. Travel on Forest Road 3615 for 7.5 miles and turn right on Forest Road 019. Follow 019 for 5 miles to the Lookout.

ELEVATION 8222 feet

WHAT IS PROVIDED A woodstove, propane stove, refrigerator, and lights, fold up cots, and a small table, and chair are provided. A vault toilet is also on site.

WHAT TO BRING Bring drinking water. Potable water is available at the Mud Creek Forest Camp—which you will drive past on the way up to the lookout.

HISTORY The cabin was built in 1948 and has been used as a fire lookout for the Warner Mountains on the Lakeview Ranger District.

AROUND YOU From the Drake Peak Lookout, you are overlooking the Warner Mountains in south-central Oregon. On a clear day you can see three states—Oregon, California, and Nevada. This is a lovely spot for bird watching, photography, hiking, seasonal wildflower viewing, stargazing, and quiet relaxing.

FOR MORE INFORMATION
Lakeview Ranger District
HC 64, Box 60
Lakeview, Oregon 97630
(541) 947-3334
http://www.fs.fed.us/r6/fremont/rogs/drakes.htm
http://www.fs.fed.us/r6/w-w/recreation/cabin/cabin-info.shtml

Drake Peak Lookout

> *"Oh as I was young and easy in the mercy of his means,*
> *Time held me green and dying though I sang in my chains*
> *like the sea."*
>
> Dylan Thomas, *Fern Hill*

61 Currier Guard Station

YOUR BEARINGS

30 miles west of Paisley and 2 miles east of Pike's Crossing

AVAILABILITY June 1 through November 15.

CAPACITY The cabin houses three to four people comfortably.

DESCRIPTION The former Fire Guard Station is a two-room cabin with approximately 450 square feet of living space. The cabin offers guests a scenic, peaceful spot for relaxation and enjoyment of outdoor recreational activities, including hiking, fishing, hunting, bird watching, and mountain biking.

COST $30 per night with monies used directly for the maintenance of the cabin.

RESERVATIONS The fee is charged per group per night. The minimum stay is one night and the maximum is seven consecutive nights. Call the toll-

Currier Guard Station

free National Recreation Reservation Service (1-877-444-6777) or make your reservations online at www.ReserveUSA.com.

HOW TO GET THERE From Paisley District Office go 12 miles north of Paisley and turn left on Forest Road 29 (Government Harvey Pass). Travel 10 miles to the junction with Forest Road 2901 and Forest Road 29. Turn left and stay on Road 29 for 2 more miles. At paved T-junction with Forest Road 28, stay to the right and go 3.5 miles to the junction with Forest Road 30. Stay left on Forest Road 30 at paved Y-intersection. One mile southwest on Forest Road 30 is a sign for Currier Guard Station. Turn right. There will be a locked gate you can open with the combination you have been given for the cabin. Caution: drive carefully on Government Harvey Pass (Road 29) as it is has narrow curves and washboard conditions.

From Bly District Office, travel one mile west of Bly. Turn right on County Road 1257 (Ivory Pine Road) which will become Forest Road 30. Stay on Forest Road 30 for approximately 33 miles. Two miles past Pike's Crossing you will find a sign for Currier Guard Station. Turn left.

From Silver Lake District Office travel .5 mile east on Highway 31 and turn right on County Road 4-12. Take Forest Road 28 approximately 40 miles to Forest Road 30. Turn right. One mile down Forest Road 30 you will find the Currier Guard Station signpost. Turn right.

ELEVATION 5940 feet

WHAT IS PROVIDED The bedroom/living room is furnished with one bunk bed set, one double bed, and a propane heat stove. The kitchen is equipped with a table, chairs, and a propane refrigerator, and cook stove. There is no water at the cabin (pack in enough water for your stay). Cooking, light and heat are provided by propane appliances. A outhouse is located out the rear door of the cabin.

WHAT TO BRING Provide your own cookware, table service, and bedding. Bring water for your drinking, cooking, and washing needs. No water is available.

HISTORY Currier Guard Station was constructed in 1933 as a field station of the Paisley Ranger District to house forest fire prevention crews. These crews occupied the Station seasonally until the early 1990s.

AROUND YOU Paradise Creek and the Sycan Wild and Scenic River.

FOR MORE INFORMATION
Paisley Ranger District
Highway 31
P.O. Box 67
Paisley, OR 97636
(541) 943-3114
http://www.fs.fed.us/r6/fremont/rogs/currier.htm
http://www.fs.fed.us/r6/w-w/recreation/cabin/cabin-info.shtml

"I have a great deal of company in my own house; especially in the morning when nobody calls."

Henry David Thoreau, *Walden*

62 Bald Butte Lookout

YOUR BEARINGS

25 miles west of Paisley
40 miles northeast of Bly
85 miles northeast of Klamath Falls
110 miles south of Bend

AVAILABILITY June 15 to October 15.

CAPACITY One to two people comfortably.

DESCRIPTION Panoramic view of three western states. Furnished with period furniture. Listed on the National Historic Lookout Register.

COST $30 per night with monies used directly for the maintenance of the lookout. The fee is charged per group per night.

RESERVATIONS The minimum stay is one night and the maximum is seven consecutive nights. Call the toll-free National Recreation Reservation Service (1-877-444-6777) or make your reservations online at www.ReserveUSA.com.

HOW TO GET THERE The final 1.5 miles of dirt road to Bald Butte Lookout are navigable by low-clearance highway vehicles—but only barely—even in summer. The road is steep, rough, and rocky in places. Leave

Bald Butte Lookout

the Ferrari at home, and don't get distracted by those lovely groves of aspen that fringe the rolling meadows along the way.

From Paisley Ranger Station, travel 0.5 mile north on Highway 31, and turn left onto Mill Street, which is County Road 2-8. Follow Mill Street to a Y-intersection and veer right onto Forest Road 3315. Continue for 18 miles to Forest Road 28. Turn left. Then, travel less than a mile to the junction with Forest Road 3411.

Turn right onto Forest Road 3411, following the sign: LEE THOMAS CAMPGROUND, SANDHILL CAMPGROUND, BLY, and travel 1.5 miles on gravel to Forest Road 450—which is just before the Whitehorse Creek crossing. Turn right up the dirt road. Bald Butte Lookout is 1.5 miles ahead.

From Bly Ranger Station, travel east on Highway 140 for one mile. Turn left (north) at the sign for Campbell Lake and proceed for about one half mile to Forest Road 34. Turn right and drive 19 miles to Forest Road 3372. Turn left and travel 10 miles to Forest Road 3411. Here, turn right. Travel four miles to Forest Road 450, which will be on your left just after you cross Whitehorse Creek. Take Forest Road 450 for 1.5 miles up to the lookout.

From Lakeview District Office travel Highway 140 west for 3 miles, then turn right onto County Road 2-16. Stay on the County Road for 5 miles. Turn left onto County Road 2-16A and within 2 miles, you will be on Forest Road 28. Stay on the 28 Road for 20 miles to Road 3411. Turn left and drive 2 miles to Road 450. Take a right and go up to Bald Butte.

From Silver Lake District Office go 0.5 mile east on Highway 31 and turn right onto County Road 4-12 (this becomes Forest Road 28). Drive on Forest Road 28 for 51 miles to Forest Road 3411. Turn right. Travel 2 miles to road 450, which leads you to Bald Butte.

ELEVATION 7536 feet

WHAT IS PROVIDED The lookout itself is immaculately clean and has been lovingly restored to its 1930s days of glory. The furniture, including a double bed, table, four chairs, and a bench, was built from original 1920s plans. These furnishings are a delight to behold and a credit to the many people involved.

Propane cooking and heating appliances are provided, as well as a propane light. There is no fridge. An outhouse is next to the cabin.

WHAT TO BRING Food and beverages, the facility key (provided by the Forest Service), flashlight with extra batteries, first aid equipment, matches and lighter, sleeping bags, and bedding. Bring drinking water, camera and film, garbage bags—the Forest has a pack-it-in–pack-it-out policy—firewood for outdoor fires, dish towels/soap, and toiletries/tissue.

HISTORY Bald Butte Lookout was constructed from a kit as an L-4 Ground-Mounted Lookout. This type of lookout was once common throughout Oregon, but Bald Butte is now one of the few in the state. The lookout was assembled for a total cost of $668. The kit and materials cost $558 and the construction costs were $110. It was assembled here in a matter of days during the summer of 1931. For the next fifty years, its crew watched over Gearhart Mountain, Sycan Marsh, Yamsay Mountain, Lee Thomas Meadow, Slide Mountain, the upper Chewaucan River drainage, and all the forested country in between.

As testimony to the soundness of its original design and construction, it is still standing after sixty-plus years of almost constant buffeting by strong winds, as well as seasonal snow and rainstorms.

A Kellogg hand-crank telephone was the primary means of communication with other fire lookouts and guard stations in Fremont National Forest. Water was hauled from Bald Butte Spring, about a half mile southwest.

During World War II, the lookout staff kept careful vigilance for Japanese fire-bombs, which were launched from Japan on hot air balloons and carried on the winds across southern Oregon. It is estimated that 9000 of these bombs were launched between November 1944 and April 1945 to spread panic by igniting massive forest fires, and thus divert America's resources from the war effort.

About 30 miles south of here, on Forest Road 34, there is a monument, the Mitchell Monument, to Elsie Mitchell and five children, who were the only Americans killed in the US by enemy action during World War II. They were the unwitting victims of a Japanese balloon bomb. It happened on May 5, 1945, when Reverend Archie Mitchell took his pregnant wife, Elsie, and five Sunday school students to the woods for a picnic just a few miles northwest of Bly. While Reverend Mitchell parked the car, his wife and the children noticed an unusual object on the ground among the trees. When they went to inspect it, it exploded, killing them all. Reverend Mitchell was the sole survivor.

Records show that the lookout was maintained periodically until the mid-1960s. More sophisticated fire detection, including aerial surveillance, electronic observation, and better road access, made many lookouts obsolete. In time, most were abandoned or, worse, destroyed. Bald Butte Lookout was rescued from a similar fate in September 1993, through the efforts of two groups of volunteers in the Passport in Time program. They, with Forest Service staff, restored the lookout to its original 1930s condition. It is now available to you, a happy outcome for this little cabin in the clouds.

AROUND YOU Overlooking the Gearhart Wilderness in south-central Oregon. On a clear day you can see part of California, and, on clearer days, part of Washington State—or so we are told.

When we were there in late August, the very last remnant of winter snow was still on the ground. The air in the glorious meadow around the lookout was heavy with the mingled scents of sage, pine and alpine wildflowers, while the long grass undulating in the breeze made the hillside look like an ocean.

To the west and northwest are Mt. Scott, Mt. McLoughlin and Diamond Peak. To the south and southwest are glorious Mt. Shasta, the Gearhart Wilderness, and Dead Horse Rim. To the east are Warner Peak, Abert Rim, Hart Mountain, Drake Peak, and Brattain, Morgan, and Avery buttes. To the north is Slide Mountain and on a clear day, a view into forever.

If you can bear to leave this place, the Lee Thomas Trailhead is on Forest Road 3411, a couple of miles west of the Forest Road 450 junction. From the trailhead the Dead Horse Trail goes south past Lee Thomas Meadow to Dead Horse Rim. It also leads to Dead Horse Lake and Campbell Lake.

FOR MORE INFORMATION
Paisley Ranger District
Highway 31
P.O. Box 67
Paisley, OR 97636
(541) 943-3114
http://www.fs.fed.us/r6/fremont/rogs/baldbut.htm
http://www.fs.fed.us/r6/w-w/recreation/cabin/cabin-info.shtml

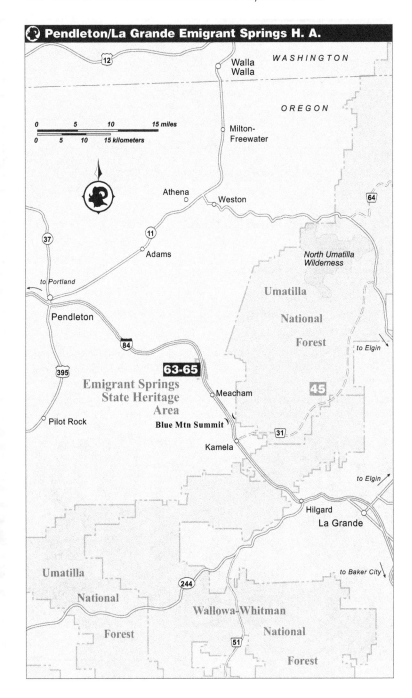

Pendleton/La Grande Emigrant Springs H. A.

12

Walla Walla

WASHINGTON

OREGON

0   5   10   15 miles
0   5   10   15 kilometers

Milton-Freewater

Athena

Weston

64

37

11

Adams

North Umatilla Wilderness

to Portland

Umatilla

Pendleton

National

84

Forest

to Elgin

395

63-65

Emigrant Springs State Heritage Area

Meacham

45

Pilot Rock

Blue Mtn Summit

31

Kamela

to Elgin

Hilgard

La Grande

Umatilla

to Baker City

National

244

Wallowa-Whitman

Forest

National

51

Forest

Emigrant Springs
State Heritage Area

"I must keep writing to remember who I am."

From *Pioneer Woman*

63 Totem Bunkhouse

YOUR BEARINGS

26 miles southeast of Pendleton, Oregon
25 miles northwest of La Grande
65 miles south of Walla Walla
70 miles northwest of Baker City

AVAILABILITY Year-round.

CAPACITY Side A sleeps four on two bunk beds. Side B sleeps three on one double bunk bed (double on the bottom and a single on the top). Ideal for families.

DESCRIPTION Recently built log cabin with two 15 x 9-foot rooms. Not secluded, but situated in a lovely park. This rental offers the charm of

Totem Bunkhouse

a log cabin along the Oregon Trail and the convenience of a full-service campground. The Emigrant Springs Totem Cabin is actually two units, each furnished with bunk beds. Rent one for a small party, or both for a larger gathering. Cooking, smoking, and pets are not currently permitted inside.

COST $20 per night per unit.

RESERVATIONS Call the toll-free Reservations Northwest at 1-800-452-5687, or make your reservations online at www.oregonstateparks.org. You may reserve cabins and horse campsites two days to nine months in advance. Check-in time is 4:00 P.M. Checkout time is 1:00 P.M.

HOW TO GET THERE Travel 26 miles northwest on Interstate 84 from La Grande and take Exit 234 to Emigrant Springs State Park. Or, travel 26 miles southeast on Interstate 84 from Pendleton and take Exit 234 to the park.

ELEVATION 3800 feet

WHAT IS PROVIDED The bunkhouse is a log cabin, recently built, and close to the campground entrance. It has electric heat and lights, and is divided into two separate rooms, A and B. Each room contains two bunk beds, and sleeps four. The beds take up most of the space. Outside, there are picnic tables and fire rings. Also provided are heat, lights, and electricity.

The park has three 16 x 16-foot corrals for horses, as well as "primitive" camping for their riders. There is a horse trail that circles through the primitive area. You will also find a group picnic area and an Oregon Trail exhibit in the campground.

WHAT TO BRING Dishes, pots, pans, and eating utensils for campfire cooking; and in winter, drinking water. Snowmelt can be used for your washing needs, though safe drinking water from snow cannot be assured, so have the means to treat it. Bedding, food, and dishes—basically the usual camping stuff EXCEPT for the tent or RV.

THE SETTING This bunkhouse is one of two structures in this book that fulfill few of our requirements. It is neither secluded nor remote and it offers little in the way of solitude. It is, in fact, in the middle of a big campground with 18 full hookups and 33 tent sites—Emigrant Springs State Park—which is beside Interstate 84, about halfway between Pendleton and La Grande. Nevertheless, it could be just the totem for weary and harassed parents who cannot travel another mile with carbound kids who have spilled yet another can of soda—though of course it is wiser and more prudent to have made advance reservations. The good news is that the park is very accessible and is almost totally shaded all day by lovely old trees.

HISTORY First discovered by Europeans in 1834, Emigrant Springs was a favorite camping place for emigrants on the Oregon Trail. It had fresh spring water, plenty of firewood, and lovely shade. (Regrettably the springs were destroyed in recent years by highway and pipeline construction). There is a stone monument to these travelers at the side of the highway that was dedicated by President Warren Harding in 1923. Interstate 84, broadly speaking, parallels and crisscrosses this section of the original Oregon Trail.

AROUND YOU You are surrounded by rich Oregon history and some of the state's most beautiful scenery. To the south are the Blue Mountains, to the east the Wallowas.

If you enjoy camping at Oregon state parks, you will find yourself near many of them, including Hilgard Junction, Ukiah-Dale Forest, Catherine Creek, and Minam. Day-use state parks in this vicinity are Blue Mountain Forest, Red Bridge, and Battle Mountain.

FOR MORE INFORMATION
Emigrant Springs State Heritage Area
65068 Old Oregon Trail
P.O. Box 85
Meacham, OR 97859
(541) 983-2277 or 1-800-551-6949
http://www.oregonstateparks.org/park_23.php

"The cost of a thing is the amount of what I call life which is required to be exchanged for it, immediately or in the long run."

Henry David Thoreau

64 One-Room Rustic Cabins

YOUR BEARINGS
26 miles southeast of Pendleton, Oregon

AVAILABILITY Year-round.

CAPACITY Sleeps four people.

DESCRIPTION Rustic log cabins, 13 x 13-foot, with 6-foot porches. Cooking, smoking, and pets are not currently permitted inside.

COST $35–$37 per night

One-Room Rustic Cabins

RESERVATIONS Call the toll-free Reservations Northwest at 1-800-452-5687, or make your reservations online at www.oregonstateparks.org. You may reserve cabins and horse campsites two days to nine months in advance. Check-in time is 4:00 P.M. Checkout time is 1:00 P.M.

HOW TO GET THERE Travel 26 miles northwest on Interstate 84 from La Grande and take Exit 234 to Emigrant Springs State Park. Or, travel 26 miles southeast on Interstate 84 from Pendleton and take Exit 234 to the park.

ELEVATION 3800 feet

WHAT IS PROVIDED Restrooms and showers are a short walk from every cabin. The cabins are furnished with a double bed, a single-sized bunk bed, a dining table and chairs, heat, lights, and electricity. Outside they offer a covered porch and bench, outdoor fire pit and picnic table, and a locking door.

WHAT TO BRING Bedding, food, first-aid kit, and usual camping supplies.

HISTORY First discovered by Europeans in 1834, Emigrant Springs was a favorite camping place for emigrants on the Oregon Trail. It had fresh spring water, plenty of firewood, and lovely shade. (Regrettably the springs were destroyed in recent years by highway and pipeline construction). There is a stone monument to these travelers at the side of the highway that was dedicated by President Warren Harding in 1923. Interstate 84, broadly speaking, parallels and crisscrosses this section of the original Oregon Trail.

AROUND YOU The Oregon Trail wagon ruts can be seen at Deadman's Pass Rest Area, seven miles northwest of Emigrant Springs State Park, on I-84. The Blue Mountains offer many recreation opportunities.

FOR MORE INFORMATION
Emigrant Springs State Heritage Area
65068 Old Oregon Trail
P.O. Box 85
Meacham, OR 97859
(541) 983-2277 or 1-800-551-6949
http://www.oregonstateparks.org/park_23.php

"The entire earth is but a leaf."

Henry David Thoreau, *Walden*

65 Two-Room Rustic Cabins

YOUR BEARINGS

26 miles southeast of Pendleton, Oregon

AVAILABILITY Year-round.

CAPACITY Sleeps up to six people.

DESCRIPTION With slightly more room than the standard one-room rustic cabin, the two-room cabin is a balance between comfort and economy. Cooking, smoking, and pets are not currently permitted inside.

COST $35 per night.

RESERVATIONS Call the toll-free Reservations Northwest at 1-800-452-5687, or make your reservations online at www.oregonstateparks.org. You may reserve cabins and horse campsites two days to nine months in advance. Check-in time is 4:00 P.M. Checkout time is 1:00 P.M.

HOW TO GET THERE Travel 26 miles northwest on Interstate 84 from La Grande and take Exit 234 to Emigrant Springs State Park. Or, travel 26 miles southeast on Interstate 84 from Pendleton and take Exit 234 to the park.

ELEVATION 3800 feet

WHAT IS PROVIDED The two-room cabins are furnished with a double bed, single-sized bunk bed, futon sleeper sofa (double size), dining table, and chairs. Also provided are a small refrigerator, heat, lights, and electricity. Outside the cabin offers a covered porch, picnic table, and, at some sites, an outdoor gas barbecue grill. Restrooms and showers are a short walk from every cabin.

WHAT TO BRING Bedding, food, first-aid kit, and usual camping supplies.

HISTORY First discovered by Europeans in 1834, Emigrant Springs was a favorite camping place for emigrants on the Oregon Trail. It had fresh spring water, plenty of firewood, and lovely shade. (Regrettably the springs were destroyed in recent years by highway and pipeline construction). There is a stone monument to these travelers at the side of the highway that was dedicated by President Warren Harding in 1923. Interstate 84, broadly speaking, parallels and crisscrosses this section of the original Oregon Trail.

AROUND YOU The Oregon Trail wagon ruts can be seen at Deadman's Pass Rest Area, seven miles northwest of Emigrant Springs State Park, on I-84. The Blue Mountains offer many recreation opportunities.

FOR MORE INFORMATION
Emigrant Springs State Heritage Area
65068 Old Oregon Trail
P.O. Box 85
Meacham, OR 97859
(541) 983-2277 or 1-800-551-6949
http://www.oregonstateparks.org/park_23.php

About the Authors

During the mid-1970s to late 1980s, **Tish McFadden** worked for the United States Forest Service as an anthropologist and historian. She worked to preserve historic and prehistoric cultural sites, artifacts and architecture on public lands in the Intermountain and Pacific Northwest Regions. In 1988, after many years of fieldwork and federal employment, Tish put her attention to entrepreneurial pursuits and founded a music business in Ashland, Oregon called Rum Tum Music Company. In addition to teaching, performing, composing, and recording music, she writes lyrical stories for children and enjoys camping in the backcountry with her grown sons and big, gentle dogs.

Tom Foley was born and reared on a small farm in the west of Ireland, but has spent much of his life traveling and working in other parts of the globe. He now lives with his son, Nino, in Ashland, Oregon, where he works as— among other things—a father, writer, photographer, and storyteller.

Walking

I have met with but one or two persons in the course
of my life who understood the art of Walking, that is,
of taking walks—who had a genius, so to speak, for
sauntering, which word is beautifully derived "from
idle people who roved about the country, in the
Middle Ages, and asked charity, under pretense of
going a la Sainte Terre," to the Holy Land, till the
children exclaimed, "There goes a Sainte-Terrer," a
Saunterer, a Holy-Lander. They who never go to the
Holy Land in their walks, as they pretend, are indeed
mere idlers and vagabonds; but they who do go there
are saunterers in the good sense, such as I mean.
Some, however, will derive the word from sans terre,
without land or a home, which, therefore, in the good
sense, will mean, having no particular home, but
equally at home everywhere. For this is the secret of
successful sauntering. He who sits still in a house all
the time may be the greatest vagrant of all; but the
saunterer, in the good sense, is no more vagrant than
the meandering river, which is all the while sedulously
seeking the shortest route to the sea. But I prefer the
first, which, indeed, is the most probable derivation.
For every walk is a sort of crusade, preached by some
Peter the Hermit in us, to go forth and reconquer this
Holy Land from the hands of the Infidels.

Henry David Thoreau, *Walking*

Index

Printed in the USA
CPSIA information can be obtained
at www.ICGtesting.com
JSHW012029140824
68134JS00033B/2964